Molière than Thou

Molière than Thou

a Gleefully Giddy One-Man Classical Comedy

Borrowed from the plays of Jean Baptiste Poquelin Molière
Drawn from new rhyming versions

by Timothy Mooney

Molière Than Thou
© 2013 by Timothy Mooney

ALL RIGHTS RESERVED

Credits:
Cover Illustration by David Jensen
Calligraphy by Debby Reelitz

ISBN 13: 978-0-9831812-2-4
ISBN 10: 0983181225
Library of Congress Control Number: 2013933633

Reviews from performances of
Molière Than Thou

Best of Fringe: Best Adapted Work.   *San Francisco Fringe Festival*

The audience is enthralled… Timothy Mooney is the real deal… A very tight performance indeed, which should be seen by any aspiring actor who wants to tread the boards.   *George Psillidies, nytheatre.com*

"Top Ten of 2006" One-of-a-kind… original, weird and seriously funny… one of the most creative and refreshing pieces of classical theatre I've seen in years… Mooney's translations make Molière's 17th century language instantly accessible. His interpretations were crisp, stylized and sang with the comic genius of the playwright's original intent. *Ruth Cartlidge, Chattanooga Pulse*

Mooney is clearly enraptured by the great French playwright… The translations are wonderful… well worth seeing, both for those familiar with the work and those looking for an accessible introduction.
          Amy Barratt, Montreal Mirror

Playwright-actor Tim Mooney has become playwright-actor Jean Baptiste Poquelin, a.k.a. Molière… in Mooney's own artful translations… ***The humanities are in safe hands this year***.   *San Francisco Bay Guardian*

Molière has never been more accessible… Acrobatic and appealing… Mooney varies his poetic, satirical and vocal tones. He's truly what the French call an *home orchestre* and, as Molière and his characters, the "music" he produces most is laughter.   *Marie J. Kilker, aislesay.com*

★ ★ ★ ★ ½ ***Outstanding***… He brings the words of this 17th century playwright to life with his animated performance... At 75 minutes long there were a number of patrons who found the performance too short, because they could have listened to Mr. Mooney all day.   *Ken Gordon, CBC*

What Mooney captures so deftly… is how skilled Molière was in painting scathing portraits of the rich and pompous… the listener can draw all the available pleasure from the splendid speeches penned by the man considered the French Shakespeare.   *Kevin Prokosh, Winnipeg Free Press*

A Molière incarnation… The 75 minutes whiz by unnoticed… I haven't found a single dissatisfied Molière patron. That says something. *Linda Harlos, CBC*

With just a costume, a series of wigs and a knack for the language he gives you a good idea of the foolishness, the conniving, the boasting and the masquerading that goes on whenever you see one of Molière's plays…
Clearly Molière lives.   Elizabeth Maupin, Orlando Sentinel

A must-see for aspiring drama students and a pleasant experience for the rest of us… Men like Mooney were born for the spotlight and he relishes every character he takes on… every unique voice he takes on fills the room.
                                            The Vue Weekly, Edmonton

Mooney needs only a trunk of costume pieces and his superior histrionics to turn himself into any number of vivid, irreverent, fast-talking characters straight from the pages of the author's greatest works... *I highly recommend* his skilled impersonation of one of the theater's most gifted and important creative spirits.   Al Krulik, Orlando Weekly

A brilliant and capable actor, and his presentation of an obsequious entertainer is superb. We all get enough Shakespeare around here, but I say "More Molière!" His innuendo is so much better.   Carl F. Gauze, Ink 19

If you're not passionate about Molière now, you may well be at the end of the show: Timothy Mooney's tremendous passion is catchy… truly fits the billing of "The Best of Molière.
                Marianne Hales Harding – Seattle Fringe Fest Review Rag

Far more vibrant; more full of the lovely ribaldry that Molière would want to be remembered for. Mooney… proves that the rhythm and the life of these works are still very much in the pink.
                Lee Howard, Seattle Fringe Fest On-line Review

Don Juan speaks like every seedy politician I've ever heard. Scapin's speech detailing how going to court is hell on earth is every bit as relevant as it ever was -- you couldn't alter a syllable. And Tartuffe -- Tartuffe is the same terrifying, monstrous figure that he's always been. It strikes me that one of the reasons that Molière's work has survived is that, sadly, his enemies have outlived him… But what he left us were his vast quantity of words… articulate, brilliant, hilarious, disgusting, despairing. There's a reason he was my hero growing up, enough so that I devoted many years to trying to emulate him. Because *we need his voice. And he's funny as hell.*
                Minnesota Fringe Blogger, Phillip Low

A very lithe, agile, and physical actor with flawless articulation. He comes off stage in a bound and hops into the seats to involve his audience. And *the Molière is brilliant*. Tim does his own translations… a seamless, fast-paced whole.   Frank Morlock, Translator/Playwright

From the Author...

It's been over thirteen years since I first got the idea for *Molière Than Thou*... thirteen years that have changed my life, taking me through a series of twists and turns I never could have anticipated.

I had already begun living out a parallel existence to my favorite playwright. Back in 1997, I began putting new words to Molière's action, adapting *Tartuffe* into new rhymed-iambic-pentameter couplets. I directed that script for Stage Two, the theatre I was running at the time, and the reception was so enthusiastic that I realized that this was a new wrinkle of my career that I really needed to pursue. While I had hitherto tossed together occasional essays, articles, poems and plays for fun and need: writing a newsletter for playwrights, piecing together press releases for a relentless production season... I suddenly realized that my writing might stand on its own, as something "legit," and something connected to the eternal theatrical muse of the man who'd produced these works 350-some years before.

And so, I wrote more. I quit running the theatre and started working my way through the catalogue of this incredibly witty actor-director-producer-playwright, seeing if that muse would hang with me through *The School for Husbands*, *The School for Wives*, *The Misanthrope*, *The Doctor in Spite of Himself*, and so on, and on, and on.

While I directed that first production of *Tartuffe*, and a subsequent production of *The Miser*, the immense responsibility of directing one of these massive events was less appealing than acting and getting to know Molière better "from the inside." Perhaps I was tired of trying to get actors to follow my instructions about the intended style of the performance, and I felt I might lead better by example, instead. Perhaps I just wanted in on the fun that every actor gets to explore as a cog in this eternal comic, cosmic wheel.

If I thought I was making my life particularly easier or less demanding, that notion was put to rest when I found myself cast as Scapin in *The Schemings of Scapin*, Alceste in *The Misanthrope*, Sganarelle in both *The Doctor in Spite of Himself* and *Sganarelle, or The Imaginary Cuckold*... all roles that Molière, himself, played when he first produced these works.

Molière, just about always, played the *largest* roles in each of the plays he wrote, responsible for perhaps one-quarter of the lines of any given play. I was leading by example, yes, but I was also occupying a fair share of the load. And, loving it.

And while I was no longer running my former theatre, they were gracious enough to host the "Molière Theatre Festival" for a few years running, and I would come back and work on these projects every summer. While we were in the throes of production, opportunities would arise here and there to do the luncheon circuit. I would go to talk to the Kiwani, the Elks, the Mooses, the Rotaries...

I was never much of a salesman. I was there to work the room for donations and ticket sales, under the guise of introducing them to the character and life of Molière. I may have sold a couple of tickets that way, but mostly I was just getting a free lunch out of the deal.

And, somewhere in there, a group approached *me*. A woman recruited me to come out to speak to the "Canadian Women's Guild." And, even better, there was a check for $100 waiting for me to do it (not to mention free food).

Wow. Nice.

This opportunity came up independent of me having any play to push on the group, but I could certainly fill the time with a thorough presentation on the topic of Molière...!

Except that... they weren't particularly *interested* in a presentation. Their response to my planned topic was less than enthusiastic.

"Well, what was it you had in mind?" I asked.

"Well, last month, we had a woman there who did "Shakespeare's Women," and the ladies seemed to like that very much!

Ah. They didn't want a "lecture," they wanted a "performance..." Hmm.

I'd always kind of looked down my nose at the notion of an amalgam of plays chopped up and exploited as the vanity showpiece of a single performer, who might otherwise struggle to get cast in any one of these roles, personally.

But then I got to thinking…

I had, actually, played many of the roles that Molière, himself, had played.

I had, actually, written the words that I had used in those performances.

Most of the people who have written English-language versions of the plays of Molière are not actors, so much as they are French Scholars.

None of those French Scholars are likely to have any interest in putting together one-person shows of their own material… nor are they likely to want any renegade actor to disassemble or deconstruct their work into a sampling of material to serve some other end.

Which meant: I might well be the only person around who had the means, the motive and the opportunity to do it.

I have developed a statement, over the years, that expresses this quandary as an imperative:

"When you find that thing that you are uniquely capable of doing, that no one else in the world can do in quite the way that you can, then you are utterly obligated to follow through and do it. Anything less than that [screws] with your karma."

I had already played four of the characters that Molière played in his career, and rewritten many of his words. There were at least eight more of these characters that had spun out of my laptop computer in recent years. I certainly had plenty of material.

But, why would Molière be performing all by himself? He had a whole troupe available to him… perhaps fifteen or more people who were in most of the plays he presented. So, why would they not be around to perform all of the roles that Molière had written for them?

Sometimes coming up with the right answers is simply a matter of asking the right questions, because, once I had that question firmly in mind, I had my answer within the course of less than an hour.

The rest of the cast had gotten sick! What could they all have come down with communally that would not have touched Molière? It couldn't be anything contagious…? Ah. "Food Poisoning!"

One hundred percent of the very first draft of this play was actually written in verse. Whether it was Molière speaking, or whether he was playing one of his characters, I had him spinning out super-human verse spontaneously (an idea I'd gotten by watching the Royal Shakespeare Company videotape of Bulgakov's "Molière"). But before I got halfway through my first test performance for friends in my living room, I could tell that going all-verse was a confusing train wreck. People needed some stylistic separation between Molière and his characters.

Several drafts later, following that first, very brief, "Canadian Women's Guild" performance, I opened the play with my former theatre company, Stage Two, as a two-act event, featuring twelve different characters and a fifteen-minute intermission that always seemed to stretch into twenty and twenty-five minutes. It was politely… even warmly received, but something wasn't working.

The intermission was a killer. While performing a one-man show was a huge undertaking, and a major challenge to my stamina, it was actually *the break between the acts* that was daunting. Having thrown myself one-hundred percent into the first act, my instinct was to go backstage and collapse into a heap (which I often did).

And then I would dread the second act. I felt dead to the world, but I had to be the most energetic spark of light in the room, even after 15, 20, 25 minutes of down-time. Of course, I would haul myself up off of the floor and make it happen somehow, but it was a shock to my system. And the play wouldn't finish until perhaps 155 minutes after it had begun.

Meanwhile, the audience assumed the opposite: "Of course, Tim needs his down-time so that he'll be refreshed and renewed to go at it again." To them, that intermission that I dreaded was some kind of a "break."

The audience of a one-person play never quite lets go of the awareness that one person is doing it all by themselves. That awareness adds to the "Degree of Difficulty" as they might call it in Ice Skating or Gymnastics. When the Degree of Difficulty is the highest, the impact is the greatest. I was diminishing the impact by spreading the thing out into two acts.

Moreover, some of my character traits were looking similar. The "cuckolded husband" types repeated through four different plays, and spinning out that particular tale was not increasing appreciation of Molière's depth and texture. *School for Wives* and *Sganarelle* were getting the better laughs... so the others were set aside, the intermission was ditched, and the play tightened to a breezy 85 minutes.

When the first run of the play with Stage Two closed, I was left with a trunk filled with costumes and the ability to drag the thing to other venues. I performed at my old high school, at a university in Wisconsin, and a school down in Tennessee. I did the thing perhaps 5-6 times that first year.

And, somewhere in there, a friend convinced me to bring my show to the Seattle Fringe Festival. "It would be a blast!" she said. "You'll love the festival and the people, and they'll love your show..."

I got in. And there were several months between my application being accepted and the festival happening.

And I started thinking about the cost of driving to Seattle, paying for gas, getting hotel rooms, and then coming all the way back. However many tickets I might sell to a few strangers in Seattle, that ticket income would not likely pay for travel and lodging.

While I had been writing to theatre departments around the country for some time (suggesting that, in addition to those new versions of the plays of Molière that they really ought to be producing, perhaps they might want to bring me in to perform), the actual number of shows booked over the past year could be counted on the fingers of one hand.

But now, I had committed to a trip. Which meant that there were very particular days that I would need to be passing through particular college towns on the road between Chicago and Seattle. Perhaps it was possible to approach them again, this time with particular dates, and the promise of a discount, given that I would be "in your town anyway..."

I booked four shows on my way to Seattle!

My next booking had been set for Tennessee... So, I wrote to schools along the path from Seattle to Tennessee.

Three more bookings on the way to Tennessee!

It turns out that any single performance was bringing in more income than an entire run of most of these productions.

This was the gig.

Realization Number Two: Usually your real gig in life shows up when you are trying to arrange for something else.

And so, I proceeded to plot out even more travel… travel that would potentially carry me through all forty-eight contiguous states twice each year: once in the fall, and once in the spring.

And that's what I've been doing for the last decade.

Which is yet another example of Tim-living-a-parallel-life-with-Molière.

Molière, whose first attempt at a theatre company in Paris was not particularly successful, hit the road for about thirteen years, touring mostly through the south of France with his company, before returning to Paris to accomplish astonishing things.

So, here I am, rewriting his words, reenacting his roles, and retracing his footsteps (thousands of miles to the West).

When I started doing this, I never imagined that I would be at it for ten years and more. Bringing Molière to hundreds of thousands of people. Driving some half-a-million miles.

Nor did I imagine that I might add other one-man plays to the mix: *Criteria, a One-Man Comic Sci-fi Thriller, Karaoke Knights, a One-Man Rock Opera, Lot o' Shakespeare* and *The Greatest Speech of All Time.* Being alone on the road, I have realized myself as the solo vehicle for my performance ideas, renaming my operation as the "Timothy Mooney Repertory Theatre."

And yet, if my life does remain true to the pattern that Molière has established, there is an end-point looming ahead of me. Three more years and I'll have matched his thirteen-year-on-the-road record.

Whether or not I end up settling in Paris to great acclaim is yet to be seen.

But, given the many refinements, adjustments and developments that I have added to this script over the years, from the broad rethinking of prose vs. verse to the questions of one act vs. two, to the reordering, rearranging, redrafting and nuance development with an eyebrow here or a pause there, the thing is ready for other people to see, for other people to read, and for other people to perform.

Last year I published *The Big Book of Molière Monologues*, a collection of over 160 monologues drawn from 17 Molière plays. Two years ago, I published *Acting at the Speed of Life; Conquering Theatrical Style*, my collection of thoughts, experiences and ideas about the production and performance of classical theatre, as seen through Molière, and through Shakespeare. If you want to know more background on the life of Molière, or on the intended style of performance for these things, I would send you there.

But some people just want *Molière Than Thou* in a nice neat package, for performance, exploration, or for reading and remembering.

I love those people. This is for them.

Break a leg!

Tim

Molière Than Thou

Cast of Characters

MOLIÈRE

&

MOLIÈRE *in the roles of…*

ALCESTE (from *The Misanthrope*)

ARNOLPHE (from *The School for Wives*)

MONSIEUR JOURDAIN (from *The Bourgeois Gentleman*)

SGANARELLE (from *Sganarelle or The Imaginary Cuckold*)

TARTUFFE (from *Tartuffe*)

SGANARELLE and DON JUAN (from *Don Juan*)

SGANARELLE (from *The Doctor in Spite of Himself*)

ARGAN (from *The Imaginary Invalid*)

SCAPIN (from *The Schemings of Scapin*)

MASCARILLE (from *The Precious Young Maidens*)

&

VOLUNTEERS FROM THE AUDIENCE

*All Characters (except for the Volunteers, of course)
are intended to be performed by the same person.*

Time: 1671

Place: The Palais Royale, Paris, France

Molière Than Thou

PROGRAM NOTES:

Molière is perhaps the most gifted comic playwright of history, second only to Shakespeare in popularity. While he is certainly well known in English-speaking countries, he has enjoyed greater acclaim in his native France, where they have the good fortune of being able to read and appreciate him in his original language. There, he is a national hero.

Much as any contemporary English speaker cannot converse for an hour without, at some point, unwittingly quoting Shakespeare, not a day (probably not even an hour) of network television programming goes by in which Molière's fingerprints cannot be found.

Jean Baptiste Poquelin forsook the cushy family business (upholsterer to the King), changed his name to Molière (to save his father from the scandal of having *an actor* in the family) and in 1643, began the Illustrious Theatre, which was anything but illustrious at its inception. The venture went bankrupt and the company fled Paris, touring the southern provinces and practicing in the highly popular *commedia* style of the day. Thirteen years later, the troupe returned to Paris, winning the patronage of King Louis XIV himself.

Over the next fifteen years, Molière, now both actor and playwright, explores farce with *The Precious Young Maidens* (1658) and *The Imaginary Cuckold* (1660), challenges his audiences with the textured modern characterizations of *The School for Wives* (1662) and *The Learned Ladies* (1670), and creates an uproar with searing social commentary of *Tartuffe* (1664), *Don Juan* (1665) and *The Misanthrope* (1666). These towering works of the mid-1660s would likely fit into anyone's list of the top plays of all time, and following the scandalous sensation that such withering satire drew, Molière satisfied himself with softer targets to finish out his career, taking aim at the doctors (*Doctor in Spite of Himself*, 1667), the lawyers (*The Schemings of Scapin*, 1671) and middle class poseurs (*The Bourgeois Gentleman*, 1670).

Molière enjoyed great success as an actor, playing the leading roles in each of his works. He knew that whatever he imagined and wrote down, he, himself, would ultimately have to perform. He was a genius of a writer creating with the practiced theatrical sensibility of a performer who essentially lived on the stage. Translator Donald M. Frame suggests that "Probably no man was ever more possessed by the theatre."

This was a man who changed the way we think of (and value) comedy, and the way the honest, ordinary man may be held above the merchants, the professionals and even the nobility. Molière envisioned, captured and introduced a startling, radical, modern sensibility to Western thought.

While his plots were almost comically similar to each other, Molière's manner and style were ever shifting as he established genres barely yet imagined... all steeped, sautéed and marinated in the juices of *Commedia dell' arte,* set at a rolling boil for thirteen years on the road.

Molière brought this vision to a world that had still not yet made the case for the importance and the moral need for comedy taking an equal place alongside tragedy and heroic drama. He established it as a force for moral good, which could shape the virtues and the values of the culture at large.

To defend himself against his detractors (in fact, everyone *is* a critic), Molière had to lay out the case for comedy like no one had up until then, and no one has since.

His thesis, in short: 'While we may all aspire to the heroism worthy of grand tragic figures, mankind is individually and collectively more motivated to avoid mockery than to emulate the noble heroic gesture. And thus does comedy trump tragedy in the course of furthering the public good, specifically because it stirs mankind to *actual changes in behavior.*'

When Molière wrote his comedies, he drained the comic vein in a way no one had before or has since. He knew better than anyone how to fill a situation with the hot air of pretension or hypocrisy, and to pop it with the needle of comic invective. Whether taking on religion, women's rights, tyranny, or the radical notion that love ought to count for more than economic interest, Molière said what people had been quietly thinking for years, through arguments that gave the irreverent comic mind the last laugh, undermining the rich, the powerful, the hypocrites, the pompous, the charlatans and the libertines. In that sense, he was the most modern of our classical playwrights.

Molière died one of the most ironic deaths of all time in 1673, following the fourth performance of *The Imaginary Invalid*. Having collapsed amid the show's finale, Molière lay dying in bed, with no priest or doctor willing to attend him in his final hours, exactly as he had depicted it, on the stage, scant hours before.

ABOUT THE AUTHOR:

Timothy Mooney has adapted seventeen of Molière's plays to the stage, seen in the United States, Canada, Scotland, Italy Indonesia and India, with many of them published by Playscripts, Inc. His one-man plays, *Molière than Thou* and *Lot o' Shakespeare* are turning a new generation on to Molière and Shakespeare, and his latest, *The Greatest Speech of All Time*, is opening up a new vision of history, with speeches ranging from Socrates to Martin Luther King Jr. Formerly, Tim produced fifty plays in five years as Artistic Director of the Stage Two Theatre. He taught acting at Northern Illinois University, and published his own newsletter, *The Script Review*. Tim inaugurated the *TMRT Press*, with his long-awaited acting text, *Acting at the Speed of Life* in 2011, followed by *The Big Book of Molière Monologues* in 2012. For 2013, Tim has decided to release parts of his one-man catalogue into the universe, beginning with *Molière Than Thou* and *Criteria*, a One-Man Comic Sci-Fi Thriller!

SPECIAL THANKS:

To Deb Pekin, *Molière Than Thou's* original co-director.

To David C. Jensen, for a brilliant illustration.

To Debby Reelitz, for sparkling calligraphy.

To Liz Rinaldi, for costumes that are practical and gorgeous.

To Leni Dyer for replacement costume pieces that have lasted for years.

To April Peterson, for ongoing support of the never-ending tour.

To all the people who have booked me and cheered me on over the course of the decade.

Molière Than Thou

As the audience enters, the main curtain is closed. Downstage Left, an ancient trunk sits, with its lid open toward upstage. Up Right, a small table holds a tattered script and a glass of water.

As the houselights and stage lights go down, lively classical music comes to a crescendo. When the lights come up again, Molière comes flying out from behind the curtain, as if pushed. Like the deer caught in the headlights, he beams a startled smile at his audience, wondering whether he ought not run away backstage, or brazen his way through the encounter. As he warms to his topic, he treats the matter as if the whole enterprise was a shared joke between himself and the audience, many of whom he knows very well.

MOLIÈRE

Good evening to you all, fair ladies and gentlemen. And welcome to… ah… Welcome! I'm afraid I'm *it* for tonight's cast! I know that you all were expecting a rather rousing performance of *The Schemings of Scapin* tonight… and I wish to God that I could give it to you! But I'm afraid there's been a bit of a crisis among the cast of this evening's performance. It seems that they've all partaken of the same sort of… *shell-fish*, as served at one of the local establishments that we players tend to frequent. Making matters worse, it seems that some of them had the bad judgment of actually… *going to see the doctor!* And, having been drained of a large amount of blood in the process, they now find themselves confined to bed, where they are to remain for the next twenty-four hours.

Now, as many of you are all well aware, there was a not-insignificant…

advance sale of tickets for tonight's performance! And this particular crisis comes upon us just as the theatre had begun saving for… *(looking around feverishly…)* a new set of curtains! And so, like any theatre at any time, we are loathe to **refund** the precious box-office income until such time as we have determined that there is, indeed, no way in which we might be able to provide our audience with sufficient *diversion* wherein they might not notice, or at least, *resent*, the appropriation of their hard-earned *Louis!*

And so, as the last man left standing – I had the foresight to eat the chicken – the opportunity presents itself to me to give you lucky people a special treat tonight! Fortunately, as both the author and the leading player in most of the works that you have seen here, the onus has been on me to maintain a large *surplus of dialogue* in my memory at any given time, on the off-chance that our good and gracious patron *(with a nod/half-bow to some unseen box, above the main floor of the audience)*, the king, should request any item from the *back catalogue* at any given moment. It seems that tonight, we will finally get the opportunity to exhaust that surplus!

For tonight I offer up to you a collection of speeches. Words that it has been my great privilege to recite over the years (by an author who has been very dear to my heart). I may well give one or two of you the chance to take on a role here or there, if only to have someone to look at, or…
> *(Wandering back towards the small table that holds an aged script)*

…perhaps to feed me back a couple of lines during some of those passionate love scenes that I do so enjoy writing for myself!

2

The Misanthrope (1666)

MOLIÈRE (*Continuing.*)
Now, over the years, I have found myself at the center of any number
of artistic controversies, and I am continually amazed at the
seriousness with which people take their comedy! I am always engaged
in the question of what does or does not make for a pleasing artistic
result, and, in fact, the action of one of my favorite plays, *The
Misanthrope*, actually springs from a critique which a young nobleman
drags out of the title character, Alceste. *The Misanthrope* is actually, a
psychological study of a self-righteous man who insists on expressing his
every criticism of the people around him, telling everyone precisely
where they stand!… And, more often than not, where they fall short.
(Walking to the Trunk; he removes a scrolled-up piece of paper.) He cannot so
much as find a single word of encouragement for the sonnet of this
unfortunate nobleman…

*(As he begins to study the sonnet, Molière pivots 360-degrees. By the time he
has completed the turn, he will be fully in the character of ALCESTE.)*

> LIGHTS SHIFT SUBTLY *to what we will call*
> "CHARACTER LIGHT," *narrowing the area of illumination*
> *somewhat, bringing the eyes of the audience in towards the*
> *center. (This process will repeat at every shift from*
> MOLIÈRE *into a given* CHARACTER; *and restore back to*
> *"full stage" during the bow/applause at the end of each piece.)*

ALCESTE
> *(Standing erect, with a strong jaw and a wry attitude. HE*
> *looks at the sonnet, and up at someone in the middle of the*
> *audience, as if he was* ORONTE, *his petitioner, knowing that*
> *he has to tread carefully around the feelings of this nobleman*
> *who is used to having his way.)*

The honor with which you endear me thusly
Is one which I would take quite seri… ously.
Such questions, Sir, are not an idle jest!

3

We all would like to hear that we're the best.
> *(Clearly, this has not satisfied ORONTE. Placing an imaginary petitioner Off Right.)*

There was a man once, whom I cannot name,
Who tasked me on a topic quite the same.
I told him that a gentleman must not
Give in to jotting down each little thought.
And while such hobbies make fine recreation,
One should resist the pull of publication.
For as a reputation each pursues,
We find we inadvertently amuse.
> *(Responding to a question from the unseen ORONTE.)*

I simply said that there is little worse
Than stigma from a limp or lifeless verse.
Although a man has every high regard,
The literary audience is hard.
> *(Again ORONTE interrupts.)*

I didn't say, Sir, that you couldn't write!
I simply said...
> *(ALCESTE realizes that he has been speaking directly to ORONTE rather than his imaginary listener, and pivots quickly Right)*

to *him*, Sir, that "You might
Consider if so urgently you're pressed
To publish where your name might be assessed.
The writers of bad books have the defenses
Of lacking funds to pay their large expenses!
> *(Almost facing back out to ORONTE again, he pivots Stage Right quickly.)*

But... you! Sir! Have the means, here, to resist
Temptation to turn out your *(glancing at the paper)* torpid grist.
Don't change the honor you're so far assured
For image of one dizzy or absurd."
> *(Turning Right again.)*

That's what I tried to tell this man, despite ....
Your sonnet? Should be... *filed!* ...far from sight.
The style you imitate is rather coarse,
And you've not yet improved upon the source.
These mannerisms, currently the mode,
Create a sort of artificial code,
Which borrows phrasings that some feeble hack lent,
Yet nature never spoke with such an ac-cent.

In these loose days, that is to be expected!
Our fathers, though more crude, were less affected.
In all our modern stuff, I have not prized
One verse above this piece I've memorized
          (Gathering himself for a "Recitation"):
    "If I was given, by the King,
    Great Paris to be mine
    Excepting but one single thing:
    This loving heart of thine;
    I would address the man, "My Lord,
    I won't accept this gift you give;
    We will not reach a fair accord;
    'Tis for my love, I live;
    'Tis for my love I live."
The rhyme is bare; the rhythm roughly halts,
But see you how it shows the feeble faults
          (Clearly indicating the sonnet in his hand…)
Of all the *stuff* that is preferred today,
So filled with words, with nothing, though, to say?

        (With a coy shrug, extending his arms, ALCESTE drops the
        sonnet to the floor, and the impish smile of MOLIÈRE shines
        out past the character of ALCESTE. Acknowledging the
        audience, MOLIÈRE pauses to bow, as he will at the end of
        each scene.)

        LIGHTS RESTORE TO "MOLIÈRE LIGHT."

The School For Wives (1662)

MOLIÈRE

Now, speaking of artistic controversies, I was to receive much criticism for my play *The School For Wives* which was to become rather a fixation among our theatrical community, as well as the public at large. It seems that our local competition, the *Grand Comedians of the Hotel de Burgogne* were to reveal me as the great "pretender to the French theatre-going nation!" ...insisting that my work was "nothing but a collection of long speeches!" (*Realizing*) ...much as you are going to be seeing here, tonight! And suggesting that my work was "lacking in the 'unities,'" which is to say, Aristotle's unities of time, place and action.

Now, whereas heretofore, I had largely confined myself to the relatively safe genre of farce, from this point forward, one could not so much as mention a play of mine...

> (*Molière never misses an opportunity to flatter his audience by gesturing at them as he says:*)

...among polite society without creating some stir, particularly as my character development had reached the point whereby some *certain individuals* began to imagine that they saw them*selves* being depicted in my work, and were to complain... loudly...! that they had been "unjustly exploited as the model!"

> (*As with all of his transitions, MOLIÈRE will, through the course of this bridge, without breaking stride, change costume pieces, taking a wig and/or a jacket off, usually draping the jackets over the lid of the open trunk, and replacing them with something more befitting of his next character: in this instance, a modest white or grey wig.*)

I was to play the character of Arnolphe who had a very particular plan for "maintaining his wife's fidelity." Convinced that the source of a woman's disloyalty was to be found in her exposure to the corruptions of society, Arnolphe was to take the most unusual step of selecting his intended wife... at the age of four...!

> (*If there is any scandalized murmur in the audience,*

6

> *MOLIÈRE will respond with a look and a gesture, as if to say, "I know! It's outrageous!")*

Taking her on as ward and locking her away in a convent in order to shield her from any outside influences, and keep her ignorant of any interests, or *alternatives*, that a woman might develop outside of the marriage! As we take up the scene, Arnolphe has just encouraged his now... *(with a gesture indicating her growth in-more-ways-than-one)* grown-up ward to repel the advances of a young suitor by dropping a stone on him from out of her balcony window! Unbeknownst to Arnolphe, however, tied to that very stone his ward has attached a secret message.

LIGHTS SHIFT TO "CHARACTER LIGHT."

ARNOLPHE
> *More pinched, and headmasterish than Alceste, ARNOLPHE immediately reads as ineffectual and feeble. His need for control is a direct result of his horrified fear of being embarrassed. Hidden behind his pretense at kindness and flattery is a bubbling pot of rage. An awkward smile gives a funny look to his teeth. He addresses a young woman in the front row, as if she were the young "AGNES," (Pronounced, "Ahn-yes.")*

It's all succeeded fully on that score,
And nothing else might so content me more.
In following directions I've expounded,
You've left the vile seducer quite confounded!
He looked, Agnes, to use your innocence,
And would ensnare to dreadful consequence,
A shameful state which none might wish to mention!
Had it not been for my quick intervention,
That man would set you heading toward perdition,
By winning war of chastity's attrition.
I know the ways of these young blades too well!
> *(ARNOLPHE will cast disparaging looks at particular audience members any time he refers to other members of the public and the behavior of which he so disapproves.)*

How quickly you'd be on the road to hell!
Oh, they've nice teeth, and velvet tongue for talking,
Vast wigs, fine feathers, ribbons, lovely stocking...!
Yet 'neath that stocking lies a cloven hoof!
And all their aim toward women is, in truth,

To make of them their victims and their prey,
Yet thanks to measures that we took today,
You have emerged with virtue still intact!
The way you dropped that stone made such impact,
Frustrating all his hope and his design…
Convincing me we two must soon entwine
A match for which you must be well prepared.
And to that end, some schooling must be shared.

> *(ARNOLPHE, who has been working his way closer to the
> edge of the stage through the speech above, now actually
> comes down off of the stage to approach "AGNES" in the
> front row.)*

That's right. Now watch me while I speak so that
I might be certain all I say, you get.
I plan to wed you, girl, upon this date!

> *(Waiting for a reaction…)*

And you should be delighted at this fate;
The honor of the bed and the embrace,
Of one who brings you this exalted place.
This will not be pursuit of idle pleasure,
For you to take or leave at your fair leisure.
Your sex depends on ours once this is done,
And though the two parts, wedded, make up one,

> *(ARNOLPHE illustrates this concept, with his two hands
> meeting with interlinked fingers, and then turning one hand
> over the other to indicate its particular "superiority.")*

One is… superior, the other… less;
One subject to the other's good behest…
And yet this doesn't quite explain the nature

> *(Indavertently, ARNOLPHE has allowed his hands to
> reverse positions, so that suddenly he discovers that the
> "female" hand is on top. Horrified, he reverses the positions
> of his hands, and slaps the offending hand away.)*

Of what a wife owes he who would engage her.
Such as… submissiveness she must afford
Toward her husband, master and her lord.
Should he turn darkened glance upon the wife,
She must look at the ground, and for her life,
Must not presume to look him in the face
Until such time his gaze holds greater grace.

> *(Noticing a group of women sitting together in the audience.)*

These wives, these days, so little understand,

So let them not corrupt you, out of hand.
Beware the evil doings of coquettes!
Each one of whom conveniently forgets
The duty that they owe unto their lord,
As soon as other interest is assured.
Do not be tempted by the call of Hell,
Out of an interest in some infidel.
Your honor won't endure the slightest soil!
Know that, in Hell, the cauldrons always boil
Where wives of wicked ways are ever dipped
When by such heady acts their souls are gripped!

> *(Realizing that he has gotten a little too worked up, in his fury, ARNOLPHE ratchets his emotions back down.)*

Your soul will stay all pure and lily white.
Yet once you misstep here, however slight,
It will become as black as any coal
And all will know this darkness to your soul,
For it will mark you as a wretched jade!
And all will flee this path on which you've strayed!
For Satan's cauldron boils without a pause!

> *(So fervently does ARNOLPHE talk of Hell that he must pause for a moment, if only to dab the froth from his mouth, before...)*

May Heaven in Its goodness take your cause!

> *(MOLIÈRE bows, and returns to the stage)*

> *LIGHTS RESTORE TO "MOLIÈRE LIGHT."*

The Bourgeois Gentleman (1670)

MOLIÈRE
Now, while I might like to perform a selection from last year's play, *The Bourgeois Gentleman*, I'm afraid that I originated the role of Monsieur Jourdain, the Bourgeois Gentleman, himself, and there are very few of his lines which might somehow be strung together to make some sort of a coherent monologue. Even if there were, those words might perhaps be described as *prosaic*, at best.
(*Removing the Arnolphe wig, and changing his jacket.*)
There is, however, a favorite exchange of mine in which Monsieur Jourdain asks the Philosophy Master for assistance with a somewhat less-than-philosophic task. He asks the man for help in writing to a Marquise with whom he wishes to conduct an affair:
(*MOLIÈRE completes his change to MONSIEUR JOURDAIN, with a shift into a ridiculous wig. As he pivots upstage, the character's foppishness is already evident through his preening and hip-centered walk.*)
LIGHTS SHIFT INTO "CHARACTER LIGHT."

MONSIEUR JOURDAIN
(*With a sense of self-importance that is belied by his lilting, mincing tone.*)
So, what I wish to tell the gentle lady is: "Fair Marquise, your lovely eyes make me die of love," but in a way that's elegant, and nicely turned.

PHILOSOPHY MASTER
(*MOLIÈRE takes just a moment to transform to the slow, staid, serious PHILOSOPHY MASTER. HE does not turn left or right but plays both sides of the conversation looking forward, with each character "seeing" the other in the audience, transforming in full sight of the audience. Thoughtfully.*)
Well, then you can say that "The fires from her eyes do sear your heart down to an ashen ember, and that you suffer night and day –"

MONSIEUR JOURDAIN
(MOLIÈRE continues to alternate between characters.)
Oh no! Not like that at all! I want it just the way that I now told it to
you: "Fair Marquise, your lovely eyes make me die of love." That's it.

PHILOSOPHY MASTER
You really should draw out the thing... a bit.

MONSIEUR JOURDAIN
No, listen! I only want those words there in that letter! But nicely
turned with art to the arrangement! Please tell me of the ways that this
might be set down, so that I might select the one that works the best!

PHILOSOPHY MASTER
*(Who can barely hide his disdain for JOURDAIN'S
phrasing... even more disturbed that he cannot come up with
anything better. Each time, he seems to have worked out a
better phrasing, but each new variation, by the end, has
collapsed under its own weight.)*
Well, your first choice could be to put it just the way you've said it:
"Fair Marquise, your lovely eyes make me die of love," or then you
might say ... "Of love, fair Marquise, your lovely eyes... make me die."
Or else: "Of lovely love, your eyes, Marquise fair... me make die." Or
then: "Your lovely eyes, fair Marquise, die of love... make me." Or yet
again: "Make me die of love, lovely eyes... your fair Marquise."

MONSIEUR JOURDAIN
But of these several ways which is the best?

PHILOSOPHY MASTER
(HE hates to admit this.)
The one which you came up with on your own: 'Fair Marquise, your
lovely eyes make me die of love.'

MONSIEUR JOURDAIN
(Exaltedly impressed with himself.)
And to think: I've never studied! And yet I came up with that one right
on the first go! I thank you from the bottom of my heart!
(MOLIÈRE bows.)

LIGHTS RESTORE "MOLIÈRE LIGHT."

11

Sganarelle or The Imaginary Cuckold (1660)

MOLIÈRE

I would like to perform one of my early works for you. Now, while I might like to make the case for some of my more recent plays such as *Tartuffe* or Don Juan, or *The Misanthrope*, as being the product of a more mature dramatic sensibility, it seems that the public... that would be you... simply cannot get enough of "*Sganarelle, or The Imaginary Cuckold*." (A cuckold, of course, being a man whose wife is having an affair outside of the marriage, the great symbol of which being the horns that protrude from the brow of the victim.) Now, over the years, there has been many a wag who has suggested that my ongoing treatment of this theme is somehow reflective of my own marital situation, having wed a woman of nineteen! ...When I was the... ripe age of forty.

> *(If it happens that an audience member reacts to this particular revelation, Molière will shoot them a dirty look and proceed to direct the remainder of this line to that particular individual.)*

What these gossips always seem to conveniently forget is the fact that I had been treating rather successfully of this theme for many years in advance of my marriage!

> *(Molière catches himself, perhaps having revealed more than he intended. Changing the subject... and moving to the trunk to replace his "Bourgeois Gentleman" coat-and-wig with a vest and cap.)*

Now, in the ten years since we first staged this particular farce, it has gone through seemingly innumerable revivals, to the point that there is no danger that I might ever forget any of the lines therein, however much I might try. For those one or two of you who may have forgotten... *(looking toward a particularly young, or particularly old audience member)* or are perhaps young enough to be making your first foray to the theatre, my character, whose name just happens to be "Sganarelle," mistakenly believes that his wife is having an affair with a young man whom he observes emerging from his home.

(*MOLIÈRE places the Young Man, passing from Downstage Right to Downstage Left.*)

In passing, the young man says to him, "You lucky man; your wife is quite a prize," a comment which Sganarelle takes in entirely the wrong context.

LIGHTS SHIFT TO "CHARACTER LIGHT."

SGANARELLE
(*While SGANARELLE might wish to think of himself as brave and strong, he outthinks himself at every turn, preventing himself from ever taking action. While the two may have no physical characteristics in common, this speech is probably an homage to Falstaff's "honor speech" from the fifth act of Henry IV, Part 1. SGANARELLE spends most of the speech maneuvering between references to his wife, assumedly off Stage Right, and the assumed lover, who passes off Stage Left.*)

He hasn't left me all that much to ponder
Such sordid singleness to his entendre!
The horns press on my brow; it's pounding, beating...
Such slurs! Such wicked bluster! Boasting! Cheating!
"You lucky man. Your wife is quite a prize!"
A prize worth quite a rise, I must surmise!
He flaunts their love 'neath everybody's noses!
Instead of hiding, boldly he exposes!
And stupid me, to stand aside and wave,
As though endorsing just how they'd behave!
I ought at least to have knocked off his cap,
Or stained his cloak with mud, or raised some flap!
I should have shouted "Thief!" and recompensed him
By raising all the neighborhood against him!
For me to take this all without a fight,
Is reckoning my honor all too slight.
What sort of man does not respond? What rube
Would stand aside, inert? An idle boob!
I'll chase him down. I'll challenge, take him on!
The man shall never see another dawn!
I'll show it's wrong to cuckold, on some whim,
A man who never did a thing to him!
            (*HE starts to exit, but returns.*)
Well, not so fast. Ought I be boldly swearing?

The fellow has a rather brutish bearing,
And he might think to vent his angry wrath
Not only on my fore, but also… aft.
I am a peaceful man down at the core,
And don't go 'round provoking any war.
The virtuous will turn the other cheek,
To men who are not peaceable and meek.
And yet my honor sees this provocation,
And dictates that I take retaliation!

> (Again attempting to bring himself to go after the Young
> Lover. HE returns.)

Well, down, good honor! Man your rightful station!
I will not stand for taking your dictation!
Say I should play the champion or martyr,
And feel it 'neath the belt, above the garter!
And gossips tell of that revenge I tried…
Well, would I then be somehow satisfied?
I think, when all is done that I would rather
Remain a cuckold than become cadaver!
What is this cuckoldry? What harm is in it?
Does it impair my health a single minute?
A plague upon the fellow who first tied
One's honor to the actions of his bride!
Why should my name be slandered and abased
Because my wife is not completely… chaste?
Since when do we let guilty party pass,
While it's the innocent that we harass?
Can one explain that odd result to me?
When one is blamed for wife's… adultery?
How can we stand for such inequity?
It doesn't seem at all… correct-to-me.
Is life not simply difficult enough,
Without dishonor added to this stuff?
There's sickness, hunger, pestilence and war,
Which on their own are ample without more!
These things will seek us out without our stirring;
Must we here pad the list, then, by incurring
Our honor's wrath at every irritation?
No! No more self-inflicted flagellation!
As it's my wife who has performed this vice,
I'll let her suffer here, and not think twice!
If nothing else, it soothes me yet to know

The status that it gives me is quite... quo!
And wiser men than I know to keep quiet
Instead of drawing notice... raising riot.
I'll smile, be more friendly, and convivial!
And not get tangled in things quite so trivial.
Perhaps the rest may laugh and talk about me...
But they'd laugh more with some sword sticking out me!
But still I feel responsibility
To give some nod to my nobility...
Fair Heaven frowns on such appropriation;
It's not a Christian form of recreation!
I cannot let this go without the pleasure
Of taking some sort of heroic measure...
I'll take my own back on him, to be sure!
I'll tell the world he's... doing it... with her!

(MOLIÈRE bows.)

LIGHTS RETURN TO "MOLIÈRE LIGHT."

Tartuffe (1664-69)

MOLIÈRE

My play *Tartuffe* was actually produced in two phases. The version which was first performed, back in '64 (…that's *sixteen*-sixty four for those of you with short memories)… was immediately banned from performance, under protests of heresy! This was a great affliction to our theatrical troupe, as we lost the ability to perform what was potentially our greatest box-office success ever, at the height of the theatrical season.

It wasn't until after five years of significantly re-working the script, all the while navigating the rocky shoals of politics, that the play was finally allowed back on stage with the full blessing and endorsement of the king…

> *(Executing a gracious half-bow to the imagined "King's Box" above the heads of the audience… and noticing that they have not responded…)*

King… Louis…!

> *(Noticing their blank looks…)*

…the Fourteenth!?

> *(Changing out of the vest and cap, MOLIÈRE undoes the cravat tied around his neck, letting it drape over his shoulders, somewhat reminiscent of a priest's stole.)*

Tartuffe is a play about an impostor and a religious hypocrite, who has very generously been brought in to live in the home of Orgon, where he promptly weasels his way into an engagement with Orgon's daughter, even as he is attempting to seduce Orgon's wife, Elmire. For once, I have the opportunity to play, not the cuckolded husband, but rather… *(pivoting away from the audience as he untucks his shirt-tail from out of his trousers)* the wicked rake and seducer himself!

(With, perhaps, greater emphasis than necessary.) Now, over the years, I have gone to great lengths to point out that Tartuffe himself is not affiliated with the Church *in any way!* And while his dialogue may smack of the parlance of the pious in order to manipulate his victims, Tartuffe is clearly *an independent charlatan! (Pause.)* I can only suggest that those who were the most offended by this work, were not those people of *(gesturing to take in the audience)* true piety themselves, but rather those very hypocrites and charlatans whom Tartuffe is intended to *represent,* who, after years of successfully manipulating their victims, were worried that they might well be found out for who they were!

> *(Returning to the trunk to get Tartuffe's somewhat ratty wig.)*

It is interesting to consider that even though this play was initially written over seven years ago (in 1664!), our *ongoing scandals* of the *present day* have kept this work just as pertinent as it was the day it was first produced!

And so, here, we see Tartuffe approach Elmire
With Orgon… gone, somewhere… where he won't hear.

LIGHTS SHIFT TO "CHARACTER LIGHT."

TARTUFFE
> *(With a powerful low, rich voice, and a stillness not evident in MOLIÈRE's more neurotic characters. By this time in the play, a more giggly or responsive member of the audience, sitting towards the front, has probably become evident, and TARTUFFE engulfs her with his attention, still speaking, for the moment, from the stage. For a high school audience, this scene may play as "clever," with double-entendres that they might only vaguely, or intellectually, grasp. However, for a more mature college or adult crowd, it might be played with more lurid emphasis to the double-entendres, with gestures that reinforce the secondary meaning.)*

Because one loves the glories of the Lord,
Does not suggest his works ought be ignored.
One should not put up spiritual fences,
To hide from the arousal of the senses.
Divine works bear our Holy Saviour's mark,
And in you lights a most auspicious spark!
In you rests Heaven's beauty, charm and grace,
That tender arm; that throat; that angel's face

How might I gaze at one built so *sans* flaw…
> *(TARTUFFE finds himself inadvertently gesturing toward*
> *his chest, and alters the gesture toward the sky.)*

And not regard the Maker with great awe!
Expressing love, both earthly and divine,
As God's self-portrait deep in you does shine.
I briefly feared that this affixed affection
Should mask a Hell in woman's fair complexion.
At first I fled from you beyond all reason.
I feared my soul might flirt with Satan's treason,
But soon the notion struck my soul most clear:
One might, to God, through earthly joy, yet steer,
Achieving passage through those perfect gates…
Arising through the glory He creates!
I don't mean here to overstep my bounds,
To offer up my heart with feeble sounds,
Nor to suggest that I somehow deserve
The knowledge of your loving touch, your curve…
> *(Falling to his knees, TARTUFFE opens the collar of his shirt*
> *to bare more of his chest.)*

I open here my heart, which you may trample,
Or but allow a taste of Heaven's sample.
I know, one scarce expects this from the pious…
> *(Still on his knees, TARTUFFE briefly adopts a prayerful*
> *pose.)*

But let that preference not incur your bias:
Amid the glow of charms that shine celestial,
I lose my modest hesitation, lest you'll
Discount my love as "Christian charity."
> *(Getting up and dusting off the knees of his trousers.)*

My pious stance is mere posterity.
The world may paint me as a soul angelic,
While I know that perception as mere relic.
What you've perceived in hot, prolonged gaze,
I manifest in humble loving praise.
> *(Gradually slithering from the stage into the auditorium,*
> *TARTUFFE works his way closer to "ELMIRE.")*

If this seems contradictory position,
Fix blame upon the object of my mission,
For no amount of earnest flagellation,
Could keep my keen desire from graduation.
Your love did spark my holy veneration,

While weaker thoughts you drove to penetra…
(Pretending to "catch himself" before completing the word… then)
                                                        …tion.
If you might stoop to give your benediction,
Relieving me of manly predilection,
All day and night, I'll gladly sing your praise,
In thanks to God, for my remaining days.
> *(By this time, TARTUFFE is directly in front of his
> "Elmire," and leans in, without touching her, to murmur in
> her ear.)*

A side note, with which you might be impressed:
In life's white lies you'll barely need invest.
> *(Noticing a man sitting with a woman in the near vicinity,
> scornfully.)*

Some other men, these days, are braggarts brash,
Who quickly turn their triumph into trash.
No sooner is a woman fondly known,
Than it's detailed, exaggerated… grown…
> *(Back to "ELMIRE," with occasional takes back to the
> "braggart.")*

Men of my sort, however, breathe discretion,
And leave behind no whiff of an impression.
As my repute I value more than gold,
No tempting echo prompts me to make bold,
Enabling me to offer you, my sweet,
A saintly safety; rapture quite complete.
> *(Sensing her resistance, TARTUFFE backs away, backwards
> onto the stage once again…)*

I know that good which on your soul is written
Would not condemn one so acutely smitten.
You know the reach of human limitation,
And might forgive a moment's… violation.
But more than any other, know you this,
No human is immune to dreams of bliss.

LIGHTS BRIEFLY RESTORE TO "MOLIÈRE LIGHT."

MOLIÈRE
As the scene draws to a close…
> *MOLIÈRE places the imaginary "Damis" in some Stage Left
> hiding place, behind the trunk or the proscenium arch.*

Tartuffe is interrupted by the entrance of Damis, who has overheard this entire conversation! Damis exposes Tartuffe to his father, Orgon, who, unfortunately, would rather believe the pious hypocrite than his own son or wife.

And so to solve this riddle, good Elmire
Allows Tartuffe seduce... with husband near...
> *Positioning the imaginary Orgon off to the right, behind a table or some architectural feature of the space.*
Positioned where he might observe and hear.
If I might just request a volunteer?

> *HOUSE LIGHTS shift from their half-light to 100%, alerting the audience that, indeed, some one of them is being asked to put their hand up...*

A woman to be subject to his leer
To read the lines and delicately veer
As our seducer makes intentions clear?
My usual victim, tonight, could not be here.
> *(As someone in the audience rises.)*
Let's give the volunteer a hearty cheer!

> *(MOLIÈRE ad libs his way through a brief conversation. He may ask where she is from, how she's enjoying the show, comment on her "interesting" costume, ask if she's ever acted before, and give her the tattered script with her part clearly marked. The volunteer will generally forget that they are supposed to be in 17th century France, and Molière is generally oblivious to modern or geographical references, and needs to "play dumb," before the volunteer realizes that Molière might only know of "Chicago" as being a part of "The New World.")*

> *(The banter is light, but always with a sexual come-on just beneath the surface; usually the less experienced or confident the volunteer, the funnier this plays. particularly as, first, MOLIÈRE's and, then, TARTUFFE's proximity becomes an imposition on the volunteer. After perhaps a minute of improvised ad-libs, MOLIÈRE and the VOLUNTEER are ready to go into the scene, usually warming into it with the explanation that:)*

MOLIÈRE

...All you need to do, is where you see the name "ELMIRE," to simply read in the line underneath it. And then every now and again, you will want to give out a cough, as it indicates to alert your husband, that it is now time to leap out and interrupt the vile seducer... before he "gets" any further than he already has.

VOLUNTEER

Yes.

MOLIÈRE

Shall we, then?

VOLUNTEER

I guess.

MOLIÈRE

Here we go.

LIGHTS SHIFT TO "CHARACTER LIGHT."

(Even as he closes in on the VOLUNTEER, MOLIÈRE turns to play out to the audience, generally catching up the VOLUNTEER in such a way that she doesn't get much chance to move anywhere. Depending on the age, maturity level, or the acting choices of the volunteer, this scene can play as an intellectual exercise or as an intimate romp. Often, TARTUFFE will whisper into ELMIRE's ear, and, depending on her hairstyle, his ploding consonants may cause loose hair to fly in front of her face. The scene generally climaxes with a "dip," as TARTUFFE supports ELMIRE in a backwards bend on "Let us finish what we started.")

TARTUFFE

My dear Elmire: a heavenly delight,
For your fair lips to give fine words such flight,
They fly about my pate, I catch my breath,
This moment I could die a happy death.
How long I've longed for kind word of affection,
Which now I feel in your most kind inflection.
But, by your leave, I pause for just a thought:
What if your daughter's wedding has now brought

You to the point of warming to this lust.
What proof have I to loosen my distrust?
It's possible that once the wedding's off,
My passions might again be yours to scoff.
I fear I must withhold my fond decision,
Till you assuage an intimate provision.
I hesitate to act on my delight,
Until my love you manage to requite.

ELMIRE
(*Coughing, to cue Orgon.*)
Such haste, my love! Allow me but a chance,
Before engaging in such hallowed dance.

TARTUFFE
So lowly am I, Madame, in my eyes,
Such notion with mere words can't be revised.
This talk of your affection lends me strength,
But only going to a greater... length,
Convinces me your love is free and true,
And that will *be* once I have *been* with you!
And though for now, I have some doubt instilled,
That doubt dissolves when promise is fulfilled.

ELMIRE
But how can my submission ever jive,
With God's dictates for which you ever strive?

TARTUFFE
Is that what bothers you? A churchish fear?
If that is all, then we are free and clear!
I'll teach you, Ma'am, that Heaven's contradictions
Give latitude to men of pure convictions.
It's true that Heaven frowns on some dark acts,
But with great men, our Lord makes higher pacts.
A pious man made study of a science,
In which, through other paths, one finds compliance,
Enabling us to balance indiscretion,
Against the zeal of one's professed repression.
I'll teach to you of science' subtle ways,
To clear your conscience and to ease your days.
For now though, let us finish what we started!

If sin there is, be it on me imparted.
> *(ELMIRE coughs, louder than before.)*

Rough cough.

ELMIRE
Oh, more than anybody thinks.

TARTUFFE
Now, if you're still concerned, know Heaven winks,
At carnal joys known quietly, in private.
Decorum is the way one will survive it.
It's whiff of scandal, draws out Heaven's wrath,
And silent sin still sticks to Heaven's path.

> *(TARTUFFE/MOLIÈRE turns from his intimate clinch with ELMIRE to draw her hand forward, indicating that she should take a bow.)*

> LIGHTS RETURN TO "MOLIÈRE LIGHT"

> *(MOLIÈRE retrieves the script from her hands and escorts her to the stairs that lead back into the audience. Just as she is about to sit back down...)*

MOLIÈRE
You know, if you'd care to stop backstage after the show... *(HE notices the audience is hearing everything he says)...* I might well give you a tour of the facility!

Don Juan or The Stone Guest (1665)

MOLIÈRE

I was not to endear myself any further to the church with my play "Don Juan," however much I might work to demonstrate the fact that the reckless libertine, Don Juan, while espousing the sentiments of a heretic, was to face a rather horrible come-uppance at the hands of death itself.

(Removing his cravat, Molière drops it in the trunk, while taking out a vest for Sganarelle to wear.)

It was, in fact, one of the very few plays in which I did not even take on the role of the title character, Don Juan, but rather that of his sanctimonious servant… whose name just happens to be *Sganarelle*. This only served to further the arguments of the pious, who insisted that my portrayal of the moralizing Sganarelle was… "limp, ineffectual and disingenuous," while Don Juan himself remained the more appealing character, who always seemed to have his own way with the most attractive women.

(MOLIÈRE does a hungry "take" to the volunteer from the previous scene, once more, as he goes to retrieve Sganarelle's hat from the trunk.)

As we take up the scene, Sganarelle has been approached by the serving man of one of Don Juan's many wives, who has come to find out the reason for Don Juan's sudden disappearance.

(MOLIÈRE draws up his sleeves, and becomes somewhat more "squat"… bowed at the knees and bent in the back from a lifetime of subservience to his master. His voice is a little higher, more strained than some of the other characters. HE treats one of the audience members in the front row as the "Serving Man.")

LIGHTS SHIFT TO "CHARACTER LIGHT."

SGANARELLE

I don't profess to know my master's heart,

Nor am I authorized to speak his part.
He sent me on ahead to scout the way,
And I have yet to speak to him today,
But let me whisper softly in your ear;

> (Working his way off of the stage, toward the "Serving Man"
> in the front row, encouraging him to lean forward...)

Forgive me if I say this too sincere:
But may I be confounded and forsworn --
(Very loudly.) Don Juan is quite the greatest villain born!
(Returning to the stage.) The man's a dog, a devil, and a beast!
A heretic at the most very least!
He doesn't feel for Heaven or for Hell,

> (Distractedly, Sganarelle gestures out with one hand for
> "Heaven," and upwards with the other hand for "Hell."
> Horrified, he realizes that he has given "Hell" prominence
> over "Heaven," and abruptly reverses the position of his
> hands.)

His heart is nothing but an empty shell.
He doesn't care how conscience grapples us
The man's a wanton Sardanapalus!
Instead of thoughts of Heaven, which secure us,
The man lives like the swine of Epicurus!
No cry, complaint, nor sliver of remonstrance
Can cause the slightest quiver to his conscience.
You say he "wed your mistress..." Fancy that!
He would have wed your wife, your dog, your cat!
And if he thought it might so serve his health,
He'd fetch the preacher and wed you, yourself!
It costs him nothing to contract a marriage.
He cares not how you might decry, disparage...!
He'll wed each woman, bourgeois, lady, peasant...
No female, fit or fat he won't find pleasant!
As long as he might... tickle on their drum,
He'll marry them however they might come!

> (Sganarelle thinks, momentarily, whether that last statement
> came out the way he meant it, and tries to move on without
> anybody noticing.)

I see that you now gape, and sigh and blush,
And yet I paint him with my lightest brush.
Were I to give a much more apt depiction
It would demand a much more vulgar diction!
I'll only say the wrath of our dear Lord

Will one day claim this soul so far ignored,
And will dispatch it to a lower level,
To wed him to his one true love, the devil!
Such horrors I see from this ne'er-do-well,
I might well wish him sent straight -- I can't tell.
Of all the evils, know by far the worst:
Is when great lords with wickedness are cursed!

> *(SGANARELLE "sees" DON JUAN entering. HE shoos the
> other servant away from behind his back while meeting his
> master, who continues in his invisible entrance to downstage
> center, conveniently keeping Sganarelle open to the
> audience.)*

Sir, it's not you I mean to criticize!
Oh, God forbid, you… know what you are doing!
And only Heaven knows what you have brewing!
But while you stand as single visionary,

> *(Indicating an imaginary "libertine" off-stage Right.)*

There are yet libertines who aren't so wary!
Impertinent freethinkers who propose
To lead the rest of us 'round by the nose!
And if I had a master of that type,
I might suggest his thinking not quite ripe!
I'd look him in the eye and say quite plain:

> *(SGANARELLE finds himself looking, not at the "libertine,"
> but directly at DON JUAN as he says…)*

"How do you think your soul might hide this stain?
Does not the fear of Heaven give you pause,
To contemplate the nature of Its laws?
Is it for you, you worm, you little freak…!

> *(Realizing that he has delivered this to his Master,
> SGANARELLE pivots stage right again.)*

(It's of this other master that I speak!)
Is it for you to jest where we revere?
To interrupt our pieties with jeer?
And just because you're set up as a peer,
With noble ties, and no professed career,
With curly wig, and plumage in your hat,
With lace of gold draped over folds of fat,
With ribbons of a flaming, reddish hue…

> *(SGANARELLE realizes that he has just delivered these last
> five lines to Don Juan, describing him exactly… turning
> Stage Right once more…)*

26

(I talk of him, remember, not of you!)
Think you, this sets you out as aught more able,
That you might be so reckless and unstable,
To act the boor, unmannered and uncouth,
Where no one might confront you with the truth?
Your servant must express with final breath:
"An evil life brings on an evil death!"

> (SGANARELLE again realizes that he has spoken Truth-To-Master, but just as he is again swallowing his pride, MOLIÈRE resumes his narration.)

LIGHT SHIFT TO "MOLIÈRE LIGHT."

MOLIÈRE

> (Changing out SGANARELLE's hat for DON JUAN's wig.)

In spite of Sganarelle's ongoing remonstrations and his iron-clad logic, Don Juan remains largely unmoved. In fact, he begins to envision his very licentiousness as a springboard to a greater grasp of power, prestige and status. It is a strategy which may be summed up in a single word:

> (Molière shifts into DON JUAN, not unlike TARTUFFE, but now with more Megalomania.)

LIGHTS SHIFT TO "CHARACTER LIGHT."

DON JUAN

Hypocrisy, you see, is all the fashion.
And with a proper show of fervent passion,
And not so much as may even exert you,
I turn this vice into a stylish virtue.
Pretending goodness is a lovely role!
Admirers will noisily extol
The many virtues of the hypocrite.
They never seem to get too sick of it!
The hypocrite enjoys immunity,
And works with sovereign impunity.
It won't take long to form a holy tangle
With party thugs aligned with this same angle.
Denounce a single member of these bands,
And you'll soon have them all upon your hands!
But even those few faithful of the troops
Are simply acting as the leaders' dupes.

They fall completely for the masquerade,
Admiring men who simply have portrayed
The outside actions of the few sincere,
And act the ape to further their career.
And in the midst of most prodigious scandal,
A pious glance, a sign, a votive candle,
Enshrouds in doubt the seamiest transgression.
It's here I mean to make my next impression,
Not to forgo my arsenal of joys,
But to engage in them with lesser noise!
And should someone discover an offense,
The whole cabal will rush to my defense!
For the defense of Heaven is a stand
From which I may explicitly command
A hatred, a harassment and attack,
With others always covering my back!
From this fell pulpit, I'll release my zealots,
To target these with insults, cries or pellets.
My army I'll effectively engage,
And my assemblage shall be all the rage!

> (Silently, MOLIÈRE signals "just a moment" to the
> audience, switches out DON JUAN's wig for
> SGANARELLE's hat, and returns to center stage,
> immediately transforming into SGANARELLE, gasping
> with horror at DON JUAN's audacity.)

SGANARELLE

Sir, it's no use. I can't control my tongue:
You have descended to the lowest rung!
There's something that I simply have to say;
It is my obligation as valet:
As that great author once said, very wisely,
I can't recall what his name was, precisely,
He said, that in this world man's…

> (SGANARELLE uses two hands, crossed at the wrists, to
> create the image of a bird, flapping its wings.)

…like a bird,
No listen, sir, I simply must be heard!
The bird…

(SGANARELLE recreates the "bird" gesture, and then
proceeds to pantomime every new item into which his list
spirals: bough, tree, tree-hugger, words-set-in-stone, etc.)
...sits on a bough, that's on a tree
Whoe'er holds to that tree, you must agree,
Must follow principles as set in stone!
And stone is stronger than fine words alone!
Fine words are spoken well inside the court,
And from the court the courtiers export
The fashion, which is subject to caprice!
Which of the soul is but the slightest piece!
The soul is what gives life to breathe its breath...!
Without the which the subject would be death;
And death stirs thoughts of Heaven in its dearth,
Fair Heaven being... far above the earth!
The earth we know is clearly not... the water!
And on the water storms cause ships to totter;
These ships must have good pilots in their bow!
Good pilots sail with prudence as their vow.
And prudence is not in the young, but old,
Who love their riches, if the truth were told.
The riches! ...Are what make the people rich!
And the rich are not the poor, left in some ditch!
The poor have needs and needs know not of laws!
And those who know no laws are beasts with claws!
And therefore, ipso facto, at the least...

(SGANARELLE loses his place, forgetting entirely where
this analogy was going. He pauses for several seconds before
reenacting his pantomime of the bird's wings, and fast-
forwarding his way through a half-dozen of the pantomimes
that followed, eventually giving up and spitting out,
accusatorily...)
You will be damned to all the devils of hell!
If that doesn't change your mind, so much the worse for you!

MOLIÈRE bows.

LIGHTS RESTORE "MOLIÈRE LIGHT."

The Doctor In Spite Of Himself (1667)

MOLIÈRE
(*Ditching the hat back into the trunk and draping the vest over the trunk's lid.*)
Following the controversies that had dogged "Tartuffe" and "Don Juan," I decided to turn my attentions toward a villain for whom everyone seems to hold a mutual sense of loathing...
(*Lifting a black robe out of the trunk...*)
The Doctor! I have found the process of denigrating the medical profession to be extremely rewarding, and have begun work on yet another doctor-play, which will be opening soon. In this one, however, I was to take on the role of the doctor himself, or, rather, I should say...
(*Momentarily pulling the robe over his head.*)
... The doctor in *spite* of himself! My character, whose name, once again, just happens to be Sganarelle... is nothing but a lowly peasant wood cutter who, through a series of misunderstandings, finds himself elevated...
(*Pulling the conical doctor's hat out of the trunk and putting it on*)
... To the role of doctor! He finds that he rather enjoys dispensing medical advice at random, all the while giving impromptu examinations to nubile young ladies.
(*MOLIÈRE gets an idea, looking up and into the audience... HE crosses off of the stage into the audience to bring up a secretly pre-arranged VOLUNTEER to play the part of the daughter. HE may pull her up onto the stage, or, if there is room, HE may pull her into the space between the stage and front row. HE asks the girl a couple of relevant questions: "You are, um... over eighteen, aren't you?" or "You aren't ticklish, are you?" Getting a further idea, he will draw the girl upstage with him to whisper in her ear. The VOLUNTEER, who has been apprised in advance of what is coming, will smile and nod her head, so that the audience knows that she is safely in on the joke.*)

In this instance, he has been brought in to examine the daughter of a nobleman *(pointing at a man in the first row to one side of the audience)*, who has been engaged to be married to *(pointing to another man on the opposite side of the first row)* a rich gentleman. The daughter, herself, however, has other ideas, and as such, has pretended to a sudden inability to speak. The rich fiancé *(crossing down toward the designated audience member)* insists that he will not marry the girl until such time as she can speak again! ...Which always struck me as looking a gift horse in the mouth, as it were! A dumb wife seems to me a double blessing, and the more fool he who fails to recognize that fact! And so, here we find Sganarelle, having administered his examination, here, rendering his "diagnosis."

LIGHTS SHIFT TO "CHARACTER LIGHT."

SGANARELLE
> *(HE speaks abruptly, as might a recent immigrant with an old-world, European accent. His comic bluff is the ancestor of the same premise of most of the Marx Brothers' comic motif. SGANARELLE divides his attention between the "FATHER" in the first row, and the DAUGHTER on stage, as he illustrates the body parts and diseases he describes with vague gestures, often running circles around the "DAUGHTER" who is unable to speak.)*

In my opinion it stems from a humor,
And from experience we may presume her
Debilitation comes from out the gall,
A state which comes from humors which we call
Unhealthy. There are vapors which arise from
Emission of the influence which drys from
The onset of the maladies which sat in,
Diseases which, you know... Do you know Latin?
> *(Whether the FATHER in the audience nods affirmatively, or shakes his head in the negative, SGANARELLE says...)*

Hmm? No? No? Not a word?
So, vapors by these humors are so stirred,
And pass from liver's region on the left,
Unto the right, where heart is left bereft.
It happens that the lungs, which are, in Latin,
"Armyan," send messages as they should flatten
Up to the brain, which, we know, in Greek
Is "Nasmus," and these messages will speak

By virtue of an artery (in Hebrew,
"Cubile") and this eventually will see to
The vapors filling ventricles, waylaid
Amid a portion of the shoulder blade.
And as these vapors... follow closely, please,

> (With each insistence that the FATHER pay better attention,
> SGANARELLE has emerged, circling around to the front of
> the DAUGHTER, with one hand still behind his back. It is
> left for the audience, and whatever the facial expression of the
> DAUGHTER might reveal to contemplate what that hand
> might be doing.)

These vapors often carry on the breeze,
And... please, I beg you, pay your best attention...
This breeze can blow a most malign intention,
Which comes from... please, now, follow this most close...
It all stems from, you see, too big a dose:
Acidity within the diaphragm…
Forms a concavity which makes a dam,
The edge of which may then begin to feel loose
As... nequer, potarinum quipsa milus.
And that is why your daughter is now mute!

> (SGANARELLE seems to have heard a question from the
> FATHER, and crosses out into the front row to pat him on
> the knee and commend him on his intelligence.)

Well, yes, that's true; you are, Sir, most astute

> (Returning to the DAUGHTER to illustrate the relative
> position of the organs.)

The time was when the heart was on the left,
With liver on the right. You are most deft.
And yet we since have changed all that around,
Advances that we've made are quite profound.

LIGHTS SHIFT TO MOLIÈRE LIGHT.

> MOLIÈRE takes the VOLUNTEER's hand, encouraging her
> to bow with him, kisses her hand and escorts her to the exit
> from the stage.

The Imaginary Invalid (1673)

MOLIÈRE

As I mentioned, I have begun work on yet another doctor play, which
will be opening soon.

> *(Removing his Doctor's Hat and Robe, MOLIÈRE will don a
> nightcap and remove a cane from the trunk.)*

In this one I go from playing the role of the doctor, to taking on that of
the eternal patient. The character of Argan, is almost religiously
dedicated to the dictates of his doctor.

> *(This time, MOLIÈRE establishes his two characters several
> feet apart, with ARGAN Stage Right, leaning on the cane,
> "seeing" BERALDE Down Left, but, whipping off the night
> cap and gesturing more freely with the cane, he becomes
> BERALDE speaking to ARGAN whom he envisions Down
> Right.)*

His brother, Beralde, creates a disturbance when he suggests that the
man's apothecary come back, at perhaps some other time, to
administer the enema which the doctor has prescribed. *(Shifting back
Stage Right to "ARGAN's position.")* Argan is horrified that his brother
should so carelessly risk medical excommunication by offending so the
doctor, and scandalized when the brother should go so far as to quote
the wicked *Molière* upon this topic!"

> LIGHTS SHIFT TO "CHARACTER LIGHT"

ARGAN

Your Molière's a disrespectful rogue,
And he may find it suits the current vogue
To ridicule our doctors in a play --

BERALDE

> *(Dabbing with ARGAN's sleeping cap, as if it were a
> handkerchief.)*

It's not the doctors he mocks, but the way
They hold up medicine in such regard.

ARGAN

Oh, I suppose he thinks he's quite the bard,
To ridicule prescriptions, consultations,
Attack our great professionals and patients,
The greatest thinkers of our current age
By putting these fine men upon the stage!

*(ARGAN finds himself looking down. Curious, he looks left
and right, and in a circle, noticing that he is clearly on a
"stage" at this moment, growing infuriated at the existential
threat of being depicted in a "play.")*

Were I a doctor, I'd retaliate,
And when the wretch fell ill, I'd sit and wait,
And wouldn't lift a finger in his aid,
No matter how he begged, beseeched or prayed.
And when he came before me with his pleading,

*(Using his cane to gesture the administration of the enema,
or the cutting of the arm for a bleeding.)*

I'd give him neither enema nor bleeding!
I'd tell him, "Die you libertine! You cad!
Go to the devil, and we'll all be glad!
That ought to teach you to make fun of us!"

BERALDE

He really has you quite a bit nonplussed!

ARGAN

The man's a stupid clown, and I would pray
The doctors do exactly as I say!
The worse for him if he gets a disease,
And has no access to their remedies.
What stupid, foolish, arguments are these!
Look, let's not talk of him, the man is vile!

(Raising up his cane as if to strike the imagined "Molière.")

The very thought of him brings up my bile!

*(With his cane high in the air, Argan realizes that he is
standing independently, revealing the actual vigor of his
health. He whips the cane back down to point at the floor,
making a whistling sound with the sudden sweep of the cane,
re-establishing contact with the ground, and removing his
night cap, as he shifts immediately into a bow.)*

LIGHTS RESTORE TO "MOLIÈRE LIGHT."

34

The Schemings of Scapin (1670)

MOLIÈRE
(*Returning cane and cap to the trunk, MOLIÈRE tucks in his shirt.*)
As you may have noticed, I have often enjoyed playing the role of the servant, largely because servants can get away with some of the most audacious trickery. And while several of my servants have been known as "Sganarelle," there has also been a "Sbrigani," a "Mascarille" and a "Scapin," as well. If these names should sound somewhat Italian to you, that is no doubt due to my own great love of the Italian *Commedia*, and one of its greatest artists, Scaramouche, whom it has been my pleasure to observe performing in this very theatre.
(*MOLIÈRE draws a colorful, oversized pair of trousers out of the trunk, and pulls them on over the pants he is currently wearing, topping off the new look with a colorful "Robin Hood Cap"… minus the feather.*)
Scapin is, of course, the name of the character that you came to see tonight, in my play *The Schemings of Scapin*. Scapin's great task is to trick his master's father out of two hundred pistoles. As the boy has been married rather badly beneath his station, the father, Argante, is looking to have the marriage annulled, and so, Scapin sees this as the opportunity to invent a non-existent "brother of the bride" who will supposedly allow the annulment to go forward, *if* Argante will settle the matter out of court! What very few people realize is that I once studied as a lawyer, and as such I take almost as much pleasure in sending up the legal profession as I do that of medicine.

Once again, I'm afraid I need to request the assistance of a volunteer…? This time to take on the role that Monsieur Du Croisy normally plays so well: that of the father, Argante.

HOUSE LIGHTS UP TO FULL.

Yes? You sir?
(*The VOLUNTEER walks to the stage.*)

35

HOUSE LIGHTS RESTORE TO HALF.

MOLIÈRE hands the VOLUNTEER the book, and engages
in more ad-libbed conversation. Once agreement has been
reached on the process of reading lines from the script,
MOLIÈRE slips over to the trunk to retrieve a second "Robin
Hood Cap" of a different color, for the VOLUNTEER, and
slip it onto his head, preferably before he sees it coming.
When all is ready, MOLIÈRE indicates, "Shall we then...?"
and pulls up his sleeves to begin the scene.)

SCAPIN
(With a swagger. SCAPIN is everywhere at once, and, soon,
invading the audience.)
I saw the brother of the girl your son
Is married to, and he seems to be one
Of those rough fellows, ever with the sword,
(Pantomimes the drawing of a sword, with which he then
pantomimes an attack of ARGANTE.)
All cuts and thrusts, he threatened and he roared,
He killed a man! he said, and did appear
No more concerned than drinking off his beer!
I taxed him on the topic, I must say,
And showed him very clearly of the way
The marriage may in time be yet retracted
(Swinging his fists dangerously near ARGANTE.)
Considering the violence he enacted
Upon the person of reluctant groom!
I then explained the courts may well assume
The father's rights, which may sway the decision,
In light of all your money, and position.
Before too long, he was so stricken dumb,
That he would settle for a certain sum.
And for the price of horse and guns and mule
(SCAPIN has individual gestures to depict most things, such
as "horse" and "guns" and "mule..." especially "mule," in
which he smacks the mule on the behind.)
He won't be tempted to some awful duel.
As long as he is somewhat compensated
He'll let the marriage be... de-consummated.

ARGANTE

Oh, no, Scapin, I'd rather go to court.

SCAPIN

Oh, sir! If you think this man may extort,
> *(Turning to the AUDIENCE, as if they were the great*
> *myriad of legal entrapments.)*

Give thought to all the law's great machinations
Which frustrate men of endless wealth of patience.
Think of appeals and writs of jurisdiction
Rapacious beasts of wicked predilection
At every stage you pass another thief
Who looks to give your pocketbook relief.
> *(SCAPIN points out particular individuals of the*
> *AUDIENCE.)*

These bailiffs, lawyers, counselors, and clerks,
Reporters and the judges; each one shirks
The fairness that they owe for slightest perqs,
And then you'll know just how the system…
> *(With a gesture to the audience, SCAPIN lets them fill in the*
> *final word.)*
>
> "…works."
>
> *(SCAPIN leaves the stage, abandoning ARGANTE who*
> *remains behind, holding the script. With each new miscreant*
> *that he describes, SCAPIN chooses a new audience member to*
> *scorn, climbing over their laps, and over empty seats… HE*
> *will make a path from one side of the audience to the other.)*

> *HOUSE LIGHTS RISE TO FULL.*

A bailiff serves a false writ on your case,
And you may disappear without a trace!
Your lawyer may be got at by your foe
And sell you out for bits of ready dough.
Your counsel might be won out that same way
And fail to make appearance on that day,
Or else he'll argue everything obscurely
And see to it you lose the case securely.
These court reporter's clerks find ways to hamper
By stealing the transcription
> *(Swiping an audience member's program, or notes for*
> *whatever review they are supposed to write for class.)*

...which they tamper.
That is, assuming that the court reporter
Transcribed it all as said in proper order.
And even having made it past them all...
The judge himself might rather make you crawl!
Some pious folk solicit him against you,
(Slapping on the knee or shoulder some older gentleman...)
Or else some woman that the man intends to...
(Sitting on, or in the proximity of, the lap of "some woman"
who is sitting near to the "Judge," SCAPIN, removes his cap,
placing it on her head, while he continues to talk.)
Signeur, I must beseech your sense of worth:
Do not get caught inside this Hell on earth!
To be at law is to be damned alive!
And I would sooner find ways to contrive
A trip to take me to the most remote
(Returning to the stage with a flourish.)
Location on the earth by fastest boat.

HOUSE LIGHTS RESTORE TO HALF.

ARGANTE
So how much does he reckon for the mule?

SCAPIN
(After a long, exasperated take at ARGANTE, pantomiming
again, perhaps with especial vigor on the smacking of the
mule's behind.)
Sir, for the mule, the horse, the harness tool,
The pistols and to settle something weighty
Between the man and his supposed landlady,
He asks in all for two hundred pistoles.

ARGANTE
Two hundred?

SCAPIN
Yes.

ARGANTE
The greediest of trolls!
Come on, we'll take this matter to the court.

38

SCAPIN

But think --

ARGANTE

I'll go to court.

SCAPIN

Do not resort --

ARGANTE

I want to go to court!

SCAPIN

But it will cost
At least as much, or case will be quite lost!
> *(Returning to the audience, pantomiming the repeated
> payments to the various characters. This time, SCAPIN
> begins on the opposite side of the audience, and works his way
> back to the side where he first began... retrieving his cap from
> the WOMAN along the way.)*

HOUSE LIGHTS UP TO FULL.

You'll pay out for the writ, the registrations,
The power of attorney, consultations,
The time your lawyer spends upon your case,
And time the advocates spend face to face!
Engrossing of the documents in piles
Will cost you long before you see the trials.
The substitutes reports, the judge's fees,
The signatures, provisional decrees,
The registrar, the warrants, verdicts, stamps,
> *(Quickly returning to the stage, SCAPIN grabs at the
> VOLUNTEER's back pocket. HE "jumps," as alerted to do
> by the script in his hand.)*

HOUSE LIGHTS RESTORE TO HALF

Upon your pocketbook will place their clamps.
And while each honest player you subscribe
That doesn't count the folk you have to bribe!

39

And here's a matter straining all beliefs:
You even pay for your attorney's briefs!
If you pay out the money now, at first,
It's only once you'll be so badly cursed.

ARGANTE
But two hundred pistoles ...

SCAPIN
                              You'll end on top,
I've worked out in my head how much you'll drop
On all the little costs of getting justice
And find the process will quite quickly bust us!
By giving that two hundred as a... giftie?
You save yourself at least a hundred fifty!
Which doesn't count the worries and the trouble
You'll find in getting through this awful rubble.
If all that you avoided was the snide
Remarks in which these lawyers take such pride,
Which they express for all the world to hear...
I'd pay three hundred just to not appear!

> *MOLIÈRE grasps the VOLUNTEER's hand, encouraging him to bow, bowing along with him, and retrieving script and cap before he leaves the stage.*

> *LIGHTS RESTORE "MOLIÈRE LIGHT."*

MOLIÈRE

(Tossing script and cap into the trunk, and working his way out of the oversized trousers, MOLIÈRE draws a more elegant cravat out of the trunk, and begins to tie it around his neck.)

Now, I'm afraid I must take, here, a moment to dispel a rather scurrilous rumor that has come to my attention. The source of our company's indisposition was, in fact, the *seafood* of a *public inn* which *must go un-named!* There is not a scintilla of truth to the suggestion that the cast of this evening's performance was caught up in some sort of a... *public brawl* over one of the *serving maidens* in this same institution! And absolutely no truth to the *notion* that *tonight's* performance is some sort of a... a *benefit* aimed at raising the funds for their *release* from *imprisonment!*

(Laughing with amusement, even as he pulls a donation basket out of the trunk. Suddenly, very earnest.)

However, as the basket comes around, I would ask that you give with all possible generosity to the... theatrical curtain fund!

The Precious Young Maidens (1659)

MOLIÈRE
Finally, I reach back to the year 1659, and yet another of my servant characters in the play, *The Precious Young Maidens*. I was to play the character of "Mascarille," who is the serving man to a fellow who has been spurned by these same "precious young maidens." In exacting his revenge, the man sends his servant to pay a social call on these young ladies, dressed... *(Putting on the most stylish of the series of coats he has worn through the evening)* in his master's clothing... and masquerading as a nobleman.

(With one final reach, MOLIÈRE picks up the last wig of the evening, a sumptuous "Alonge" wig, with curls that reach down over the shoulders. He puts the wig on while facing away from the audience, but by the time he has pivoted to face forward, he has become MASCARILLE, a self-indulgent, self-important impostor, who preens and displays everywhere he goes. He is most likely a parody of the famous overblown actor, "Montfleury," one of Molière's rivals, a player with the **Grande Comedians** *who is likewise mocked for his puffery in the play, "Cyrano de Bergerac.")*

LIGHTS SHIFT TO CHARACTER LIGHT.

MASCARILLE
(Picking out two young women, on opposite sides of the audience, to treat as the two "Precious Young Maidens," he will – remaining always on the stage – deliver a couple of lines to one woman, before reversing his field to cross toward the other, eyeing each as if she were his special girlfriend.)
It is a shame, quite true, not to be first
To know each thing composed in prose, or versed.
But do not fear, my heart for you commits
To set up an Academy of Wits!

I promise there won't be the slightest scrap
Of verse in Paris which won't find your lap.
In fact, myself, I dabble here and there
When I've the mood to trifle and to dare.
There are two hundred songs of my composure,
Next to my sonnets, gaining broad exposure.
A thousand epigrams and madrigals,
Not counting prose caricatures[1] and riddles.
Caricatures are never really quite
As simple to compose as someone might
Suppose. But I will show you some of mine
Which you may find quite deep in their design.
    (As if one of the MAIDENS has complimented his riddles.)
Is it the riddles that you find most charming?
Ah! Those can be complex and quite disarming.
But madrigals are what I'm famous for!
Why even now, I'm working out a score
For madrigal of history of Rome!
Ah! In my heart that work will have its home!
You'll have a copy once I've had it printed,
I promise you, as soon as it's been minted,
I'll bring you one bound in the finest leather.
You see, I have to throw these things together
To please the booksellers who get upset
When they can't sell the latest thing to get.
    (With sudden inspiration.)
But I must tell of an improvisation
Which I made up upon an inspiration.
Just yesterday, while visiting a Duchess,
Who loves this sort of writing, insomuch as
I wrote it for her, right there, on the spot.
Improvisations are the breath of thought!
Do listen while I work through this convention;
I beg you, give me your most rapt attention!

---

[1] When pronounced as *"caRICaTURES"*, this line stays in line with the iambic meter, and also makes Mascarille seem that much more affected.

(While MASCARILLE's attitudes have not lacked for exaggeration in any way, here he goes over the top, with gestures that might rival the depictions on a Grecian urn, and even hitting himself on the chest to act out "hit me... hard.")

Oh! Oh! I contemplated here completely off my guard!
With nothing else about or near, it quickly hit me, hard...
Your eye, so sly, I did espy; with speed beyond belief
You stole my heart and now I cry:
"Stop thief! Stop, thief! Stop... thief!"

(MASCARILLE cannot resist overstating the drama, by taking an added pause before the final "thief!")

Did you see how I started it? "Oh! Oh!"

(Each repetition of "Oh! Oh!" has its own obligatory pose... as does each phrase that he revisits from this poem.)

Like something frightful, startling, you know?
"Oh! Oh!" It's almost like a man who found
Some something that made him release a sound!
"Oh! Oh!" he says. Discovery! Surprise!
Oh, yes. "Oh! Oh!" gives it a gallant guise.
Indeed it does! I'd rather those "Oh! Ohs!"
Than any epic poem I'd compose!
But how about "I contemplated here?"
"I contemplated here," as free from fear.
"I contemplated here," no pain, no doubt,
"Completely off my guard:" no cause to shout!
"Completely off my guard," just like a sheep!
"It quickly hit me hard." It is to weep!
"It quickly hit me hard." As if to say
That there was pain in my delight that day!
"Your eye, so sly, I did espy..." How's that?
Does that not keep the verse from reading flat?
What do you think? Is it not excellent?
"Espy," to look; to sneak a peek. I meant
To summon up a mouse who sees a cat...

(As if one of the MAIDENS has reached the same conclusion.)

The very image! Yes, you noticed that!
"With speed beyond belief," just to convey
The quickness with which all this came in play!

44

"You stole my heart:" to take, to snatch, to plunder.
And tell me now: did you catch this, I wonder?
I finished off, "Stop thief! Stop thief! Stop... thief!"
Would you not hear this with the firm belief
It's shouted by a man now in the chase
To catch a thief who runs a faster pace?
As though the man had stolen of his chief
Possession, thus: "Stop thief! Stop thief! Stop... thief!"
I must say that it's brilliantly deposed!
I'll sing it to the air that I've composed!
What, music? Study? Me? No, not a bit.
You must know that a noble must acquit
Himself with quality's true ring,
By knowing all, but not to learn a thing.
You must have known that. Obviously, yes?
Do tell me if it suits you more or less.
Ahem! Ahem! La-la! La-la! La-la!
I beg that you forgive my furtive "Caw."
The harsh brutality of this wet season
Quite violates my voice beyond all reason!
No matter! 'Tis a lilting folksy air,
And here, 'twixt friends, such discord we might dare.

        (Singing.)
Oh! Oh! I contemplated here completely off my guard
With nothing else about or near, it quickly hit me hard
Your eye, so sly, I did espy; with speed beyond belief
You stole my heart and now I cry...
"Stop thief! Stop, thief! Stop... thief!"

        (If the AUDIENCE should break into applause,
        MASCIRILLE responds as if the two ladies were clapping for
        the song.)
And is this thought not elegantly tuned?
(Singing.) "Stop thief!" And then as one who feels a wound:
(Singing again.) "Stop thief!" And then, now running out of breath:
(Singing one, inevitable, final time.)
"Stop... thief!" A small collapse. A little death.
It's as to know the height of all great heights!
The highest height; a height which may ignite
A high-ness over other elevations!
It's marvelous. I am in palpitations!

It leaves me breathless, buoyant and yet burning.
It's inborn. With no study and/or learning.
              (Shifting his tone, slightly.)
Fair ladies, if you'd hear my fond proposal
I am hereafter at your fair disposal
To take you to a play, if you desire.
There is a playwright who I most admire,
Whose work is in rehearsal. I was hopin'
That you might come with me to see it open!
You must come with! You cannot here refuse!
I must however beg that you'll excuse
If I clap with conviction and with vigor.
I told the author I would be a figure
Pronounced in acclamation of his craft!
Just as at other shows I cheered and laughed!
Now that you know, you must make your design
To raise a cry at every single line!
You know, I too have penned a little masque.
              (As if one of the MAIDENS has asked the question…)
What troupe!? Oh, my! Oh, dear! Oh, need you ask?
The *Grand Comediens* of the *Hotel*
Du Bourgogne, of course. They so excel,
No other troupe around might so succeed
In doing justice to the words they read.
Those other troupes but copy… after nature!
While the Comedians cry out with rage, or
              (Rolling the "R" of "trill," and taking a special pose…)
Make all their verses trill, and then they wait
For each reaction they anticipate…
To cue the audience to laugh or cheer!
For, how else will you know what you might hear
If they don't let you know that it's now time
To make some noise, or to cry out, "sublime!"
Oh, yes. That is the way to tell the crowd
The beauty of a work both clear and loud.
Such things are valued only in perspective
Of how the players make it more… effective!

              LIGHTS RESTORE "MOLIÈRE LIGHT."

    MOLIÈRE bows. HE interrupts the applause to say…

46

MOLIÈRE

I'd like to thank each and every one of you for coming tonight, and to thank you even more... for staying! It is my great honor to perform for you from time to time, and no one is happier than I to be able to carve a living from this most unsavory vocation. If I have managed to divert you from the daily cares which are so much more important than the frivolity which I perform upon the stage, then I shall count myself as both lucky and successful.

Beyond any personal satisfaction, however, I count it as a great victory over vice to be able to transform wickedness into the object of your laughter. For a man may well allow himself to be scorned, but not mocked. He may be willing to be evil, but never ridiculous.

I would only ask that you come back again some night when we are, as they say... fully staffed!

As long as you keep coming to see us, my company will continue to perform... given, that is, the blessings of health, good digestion, and freedom from legal intervention... which is my great wish to each and every one of you here tonight! Thank you.

THE "LIVELY CRESCENDOING CLASSICAL MUSIC" FROM THE
PLAY'S OPENING REPEATS.

MOLIÈRE bows to the center of the house, to house right, and house left, before turning toward the curtain through which he was flung at the beginning of the play.

LIGHTS START TO FADE, AND THEN RESTORE.

MOLIÈRE pivots, and returns downstage, removing the MASCARILLE wig, and bowing, this time, as THE PERFORMER, himself. With a final "kiss," THE PERFORMER exits.

LIGHTS FADE TO BLACK, HOUSE-LIGHTS RESTORE, THE PRE-SHOW SETTING RESTORES.

Also Available from the TMRT Press!

CRITERIA
A One-Man, Comic, Sci-Fi Thriller!

"4 Stars" "An *engaging and brilliant* performance."   *Edmonton VueWeekly*

"A" Timothy Mooney's one-man show is *provocative, funny, thoughtful, shocking and compelling*. Stuff like this is what the fringe is all about. See it."
Quentin Mills-Fenn, Winnipeg Uptown

"It's a sci-fi action flick, a thriller, a mystery and a road movie all boiled into a riveting one-man show… The intrigue culminates in *an edge-of-your-seat finale* in which the terrorist quite literally holds the fate of America in his hands."
Cheryl Binning, Winnipeg Free Press

"A consummate story-teller. I left the theatre with the feeling that I could listen to him tell a story about almost anything... Mr. Mooney took me somewhere I never thought I would go. *Criteria* was not without comedy either. On his journey, the terrorist enters a diner where he encounters friendly small-town locals. His shock and horror at the decadence of a society where a waitress calls everyone "honey" *almost brought the house down...*"
Stacy Rowland, TheatreSeattle.com

"When was the last time you attended a Fringe show where, all around you, audience members were literally leaning forward in their seats, virtually mesmerized and determined not to miss a single word? It happened the other afternoon with *Criteria*, a very clever cautionary science fiction tale… *One of the best and most original things in Fringe 2006.*"*Janice Sawka, Jenny Revue*

"The world the play creates is one that any society can be reflected in... *It approaches the arena of politics more successfully than any other show* I've seen in this Fringe, because it does it through *metaphor* rather than through *preaching*. It's smart, it's nuanced, I loved it -- and everybody needs to see it... Don't let it slip away.   *Phillip Low, Fringe Blogger*

"Timothy Mooney's epic one-man journey into a possible future carries with it *wonderful humor, dark speculation, and a damn great time*… It will leave you thinking about the themes for a long time."*Kale Ganann (On-line Review)*

"*Criteria should be performed for corporate executives or at political gatherings and then discussed all night.*"
George Savage, Playwright, (On-line Review)

TMRT Press, PO Box 638, Prospect Heights, IL 60070 * www.timmooneyrep.com

"*Criteria* is a gem, and should definitely be at the top of your To-Consider List… bright and engaging… ***fantastical yet so incredibly, and poignantly, timely***. Skilled storytelling and clever, intricate physicality."
Leigha Horton, On-line Review

"***One Man Apocalypse!***" "A sci-fi suspense solo show with funny moments… I enjoyed this show immensely… There's not a lot of optimism in Mooney's show (though there's plenty of apocalypse-relieving comedy), but that's the way I like it."
Courtney McLean, On-line Review

"As in good theater throughout history, Mooney has created something wonderfully uncommon from apparently prosaic materials… The language in this play is ***astonishing… pulling us along, off-balance and breathless with incomprehension*** … alternating between chortles and gasps. … If I laughed, it would have to have been the laugh of catastrophe: giddy with hopelessness… Mooney creates an adrenalin rush, his delivery racing along with the momentum of the train we see all too clearly… Whether you want a punch in the old ideological stomach, or just a really exciting evening of virtuoso theater, see *Criteria*." *Richard Greene, Georgia College & State University*

"***A comic espionage sequence Woody Allen might have written***. And all for the price of a one-man show… In his confident hands, the drama unfolds at a captivating pace and the dark comedy crackles."
Fringe Review Rag, Seattle 2003

"***The action is exciting, the consequences chilling and the story telling superb***."
Carl Gauze, Ink 19

"Very compelling… ***Hard to explain but easy to enjoy***."
Bret Fetzer, The Stranger Weekly Magazine

"He's a very good actor, with a good ear for dialogue and scenes, and he makes this ambitious notion work…"
Roger Moore, Orlando Sentinel

"***This isn't the idealistic 24th century predicted in Star Trek***! …I find myself laughing out loud, again and again. I'm amazed by the acting and the storytelling… I love it."
On-line Review

"***So much suspense I couldn't believe it was a one-man show***!"
Theatre Student (Rocky Mountain Theatre Festival)

"A futuristic, sci-fi conspiracy thriller that ***will have you on the edge of your seat***… an adventure that will satisfy the most ardent fans of the sci-fi genre.
Ken Gordon, The Jenny Revue

TMRT Press, PO Box 638, Prospect Heights, IL 60070 * www.timmooneyrep.com

The Big Book of Molière Monologues

Hilarious Performance Pieces From Our Greatest Comic Playwright

(From the Preface) "Molière's lines, penned in Classical French over three centuries ago found exuberant reaffirmation in Tim's smooth and stylish English translation... Tim's high esteem and compassion for the greatness and comic genius of Molière is singular... His book of monologues is a masterwork. It represents years of creativity, resolve and follow-through. *I've never seen a better compilation.*"

William Luce, Author, The Belle of Amherst, Barrymore, The Last Flapper

"*Offers more than the title would suggest.* True, there are 160 or so of Molière monologues in new, rhymed iambic pentameter versions by Mooney, taken from Molière's plays... But he also provides plot summaries and contextual information for each piece, as well as an introduction to the life and work of Molière, guides to the performance of classical verse monologues and stopwatch timings of each piece for audition purposes."

Stage Directions Magazine

A must-read for Molière's fans and neophytes; While having the privilege to see Tim Mooney on stage performing his show *Molière Than Thou* is a wonderfully exhilarating treat, his book of translations is a riveting introduction to Molière and his work... incredibly faithful to the spirit of the plays, requiring much creativity on the part of the translator. Indeed, Mooney was able to put into verse even those works that had been originally written in prose and the effect is outstanding. *Pascale-Anne Brault, DePaul University*

Mr. Mooney has presented *Molière Than Thou*, his performance opus on the French actor/playwright, for many, many years at high schools, colleges, universities, and theaters of all sizes. This newest text is *the best of his teachings, lectures, and demonstrations in print form.* While there is no substitute for seeing Mr. Mooney perform live, this is certainly a terrific companion piece to his stage work. Mooney's exhaustive research, scholarship, and experience performing the plays of Jean-Baptiste Poquelin has made him one of the world's leading experts on Molière. *The Big Book of Molière Monologues* encapsulates much of that research and scholarship and is invaluable to anyone interested in the "nuts and bolts" of 17th century French Comedy traditions as well as an understanding how these works would have been performed. My best advice: buy this book and then bring Mr. Mooney to your institution or venue to see him bring the book to life!

Aaron Adair, Southeastern Oklahoma State University

TMRT Press, PO Box 638, Prospect Heights, IL 60070 * www.timmooneyrep.com

For those who study and perform the works of Molière and even Big Bill *this book is a must*. It takes you step by step through everything you need to know to become better at the craft, better at the art of performance.
Charley Ault, Director, Players Guild of the Festival Playhouse

I first saw Mr. Mooney perform his one man show, *Molière Than Thou*, at my college in the fall. After his performance had me gripping my sides, I decided that I had to delve further into the author of Molière. Before Mr. Mooney's performance, I knew neither hide nor hair of Molière, but I soon found myself enthusiastically reading biographies of him and his plays; I was eager to have more. This book provided me *the perfect accompaniment to my study of Molière* - it has a fabulous collection of some of Molière's most hilarious pieces written creatively for the current actor. The book not only worked well for me with my Molière quest, but also provides a large source of audition pieces. The book covers a broad sweep of Molière's plays and gives descriptions about each character and piece presented... This book can help you find the perfect monologue before you go searching through every single play out there. Overall, a wonderful book that presents truly some of the funniest pieces I have read. Enjoy!
Sean B. (On-Line Review)

Tim Mooney has created *an elegantly simplistic highway of understanding*, from the basic description of iambs to the delivery of easily understood, and laughed out loud at, skillfully constructed verse. The key to excellent verse is the simultaneous application of cleverness in a most academic and streetwise manner. Tim does this expertly. Double entendre is a staple by which we all find ourselves thoughtfully smiling or laughing out loud. *Merci, Jean-Baptiste.* Much of Tim's experience shines through in a scholarly manner... *The Big Book* is a must read for any serious French teacher or student of French. To understand Molière is to reach down into our inner being so as to discover and understand ourselves when not fettered by silly political correctness... or assisted by a shrink! Tim's *Big Book* facilitates this in a very American, in your face way. If you don't like Molière or Mooney when you have completed this book, you could not have liked Mad Magazine or the edginess of the old Saturday Night Live (the current one lacks the verve and creativity of the original). So if you are of that ilk, I trust you have read this review before buying it, so my advice is, don't bother, you are incorrigible and not worthy. If however, I've piqued your interest, dive into it... naked, with a glass of red wine and savor it. After you've done that it will be the morrow; so shower, don your clothes and read in earnest! You will be delighted, fulfilled and even a bit smarter in the timeless clever ingenuity of Molière and Mooney's genius manner of bringing this genre to life!   *John Paul Molière, Hume, Virginia*
(Yes, that's right; my name is Molière, it's not a misprint.)

TMRT Press, PO Box 638, Prospect Heights, IL 60070 * www.timmooneyrep.com

Also Available from the TMRT Press!
Acting at the Speed of Life
Conquering Theatrical Style

A unique 'how to' book offering a refreshing and highly practical approach… No nonsense steps to approach the demands of stylized acting that will be of essential value… Directors and teachers of acting will also find Mooney's book an essential resource… I recommend this exceedingly valuable book which, to be sure, will inspire actors to approach stylized theatre with the spirit of fun and style.   *James Fisher, Theatre Library Association's "Broadside"*

Author Timothy Mooney takes on the challenges of asides, soliloquies and rhetorical speech. He offers tips on memorizing lines, incorporating the "stuff" of historical style, and going beyond naturalism and realism as it suits the playwright's intent. *Nicely done.*   *Stage Directions Magazine*

Not just your average acting book: The book combines a comprehensive understanding of modern "method-based" performance styles with a reflection back to an older system that apprenticed young actors into a troupe, and gave them the basic skills needed to survive as theatre professionals. Powerful and empowering… it's necessary for every serious actor's shelf.
     Dennis Wemm, Glenville State College

A practical, informative and entertaining read! A very "nuts-and-bolts" approach to acting the Classics. His insight into the Shakespearean character alone is worth the price, but he provides useful and thoughtful analysis into Molière, Chekhov, and other playwrights' works as well. I have and would recommend this to the casual or avid theatergoer, the theatre educator, and the performer who desires to know more about how characters are brought to life.
     Aaron Adair, Southeast Oklahoma State University

The hardest-working book in my life of teaching acting to high school students… Results are seen instantaneously… From the basics of memorization to the clearing of the cobwebs surrounding the classics, the book does it all with grace and great humor. The book delivers. I highly recommend it.
     Claudia Haas, Playwright for Youth/Artist in Residence, Twin Cities

Terrific… Replete with incisive, clear-headed accessible advice and information. In my view it is *the clearest and most comprehensive work for the community and student actor written today.*
     Dr. Christian H. Moe, Southern Illinois University

One performance with Tim equals a week of teaching and a lifetime of appreciation.   *Michael Stiles, Theatre Teacher Musselman High School*

TMRT Press, PO Box 638, Prospect Heights, IL 60070 * www.timmooneyrep.com

A thunderous success! When, after guiding my cabaret class through your "Exercise," they returned to their songs and took the text out to perform as a monologue, their readings were inspired and wonderful! Their songs came alive with nuance and subtle interpretive freedom. They were humblingly beautiful, startlingly authentic, and persuasively convincing.

Loren F. Salter, Artistic Director and Performance Coach

Wow... what a great text... I participated in the exercise where Mr. Mooney took two young women from the audience and asked them to perform a short dialogue from a Molière play. After a slight adjustment from Mr. Mooney, the two performers lit the room on fire!... This is probably the most accessible approach to classical style that I have ever seen.

Celi Oliveto, Master of Letters/MFA Candidate, Mary Baldwin College

Highly recommended. A treasure trove of tips–useful not only to actors and educators, but also to directors, producers, and writers. The section on Shakespeare alone is worth the price of the book. Mooney's enthusiasm throughout is absolutely contagious.   *V.Z. Daly, Playwright, New York, NY*

This could be the modern manual for the Director and the Actor. Written with the insight of Hagen, Adler, and Spolin... A fun romp, but more than that... a must read!   *Charley Ault, Director, Players Guild of the Festival Playhouse*

The audience who cheered his *Molière than Thou* should appreciate Tim's new book... It goes from basics to advanced-but-de-mystified info on plays by Shakespeare and Molière.   *Marie J. Kilker; Aislesay.com*

The director was loving and laughing at my character and I KNOW your insights contributed to that. I made bold choices--getting the character into my whole body, having FUN!!!   *Betty Anderson, Actress*

One feels the benefits almost instantly; in contrast, when I read some, the vibe is, "you must spend years doing just what I say." Yet when you talk about Shakespeare and pausing too long, for example, just by taking that great insight to heart you can see immediate improvement. These little bits of professional wisdom that you spread throughout are so useful and interesting... You managed to make learning fun.   *Tony Osborne Gonzaga University*

Required summer reading for my Advanced Drama students. The obvious skill and experience you share will be invaluable… "The best acting workshop we never attended."   *Janet Henke, Acting Teacher, Oak Ridge High School*

Communicates with clarity, wisdom and practicality. This text belongs in every theatre artist's bookbag.   *Jeff Barker, Northwestern College*

The advanced students are really hungry for this kind of information and NO other book I've read captures these simple tasks that are so important. I would recommend every acting student to have this book.

Janice Fronczak, University of Nebraska-Kearney

TMRT Press, PO Box 638, Prospect Heights, IL 60070 * www.timmooneyrep.com

Made in the USA
Columbia, SC
08 June 2024

36373771R00041